CERAMIC
STYLE

CERAMIC STYLE

MAKING AND DECORATING PATTERNED CERAMIC WARE

JOHN HINCHCLIFFE & WENDY BARBER

PHOTOGRAPHY BY GEORGE WRIGHT

CASSELL

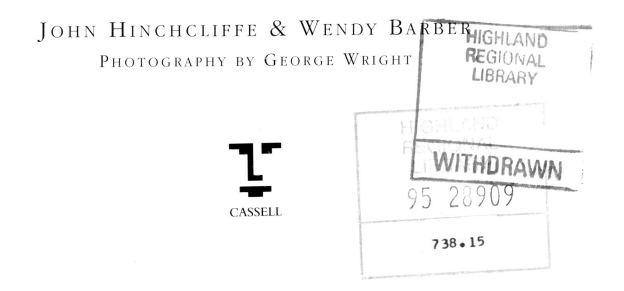

FOR GEORGIA

First published in the UK in 1994
by Cassell
Villiers House
41/47 Strand
London
WC2N 5JE

Distributed in the United States by
Sterling Publishing Co. Inc.
387 Park Avenue South, New York, NY 10016-8810

Distributed in Australia
by Capricorn Link (Australia) Pty Ltd
2/13 Carrington Road
Castle Hill
NSW 2154

British Library Cataloguing-in-Publication Data
A catalogue record for this book is available from the British Library.

ISBN 0-304-34392-7

Printed and bound in Italy

CONTENTS

FOREWORD BY SIMON OLDING 8

INTRODUCTION 10

ONE
STARTING IN CERAMICS 22

TWO
INSPIRATION & INFLUENCES 30

THREE
RAW MATERIALS 44

FOUR
MAKING PLATES & TILES 50

FIVE
TECHNIQUES FOR APPLYING PATTERN 76

SIX
THEMES & PROJECTS 104

FUTHER READING 156

SUPPLIERS 157

INDEX 158

ACKNOWLEDGMENTS

Hinchcliffe and Barber would like to thank the following people for
their help in compiling this book:

Margaret Barron
David and Sarah Burnett
Lesley Knox
Edmund Sayer
Rupert and Susie Lascelles
Ian Watts
Mrs McCraith
Polly and Jonathan Tommey
James Barber
Rosie Barber
Harriet Barber
Frances and Ian Huxley
Alexander and Flora Skeaping
Françoise and Bertrand Lucas
Claudine Renouf
Ian Harper
Hand and Partners
Joanna Laidlaw
The Derbyshire Handmade Brick and Tile Company
Pottery Crafts
Frank Herring of Dorchester
Simon Olding
The staff of the Russell-Cotes Museum, Bournemouth
The Salisbury Museum
Mary Alexander
Michelle Horscroft
Toto and Kit Wordsworth
Philipa Sayer
Anni Partridge
Jackie Cole
Chris Fagg and his team at Cassell

OPPOSITE: LATE SUMMER FLOWERS IN A WHITE FLOWER JUG.

FOREWORD

In 1983 Hinchcliffe and Barber held their first joint exhibition of ceramics at the Salisbury Arts Centre. Wendy Barber showed textile hangings and watercolours and John Hinchcliffe a powerful range of sponged blue-and-white earthenware. The exhibition was an instant critical and commercial success and established for the artists an immediate and powerful reputation as ceramicists. In addition, commentators of the exhibition proposed that Hinchcliffe and Barber had created a niche in the market for domestic tablewares. This was pottery which, for all the nineteenth-century techniques, looked fresh and contemporary. Hinchcliffe and Barber prepared very carefully for the exhibition, as they do for all of their displays. The art of exhibition is not, for these artists, a simple matter of dressing a plinth attractively or arranging a wall hanging with discretion. The artists are in search of more than visual gloss; they are in search of a style which best reflects their ideas.

Hinchcliffe and Barber's ceramics, from the earliest studio spongeware to the latest lean design for the commercial factory, is instantly recognisable. This must be due in part to their extraordinarily swift assimilation of the craft and the self-confidence in their creative ability. It seems strange to recall that neither artist had worked in the medium until very shortly before the Salisbury exhibition. The signature of a Hinchcliffe and Barber pot is primarily a matter of simplicity of shape, strong colour and sophisticated, rurally-inspired repeat images. Hinchcliffe's eye for a design and his gift for painting on pottery mark out the ceramic work of the partnership with distinction and visual presence. Their work is nearly always purely functional, though there are 'art-series' such as the tropical bird plates which are conceived primarily as ceramic paintings.

Hinchcliffe and Barber's place in the history of twentieth-century British ceramics is already assured. They have helped to redefine in their own distinctive style that area of ceramic work which lies in between pure studio pottery and mass-produced domestic ware. This reputation has been born out of a great creative energy as well as a reaction to the extremes of ceramic production. They are as nervous of what they view as the potential preciousness of 'art pottery' as they have been scathing about the standard of much commercial work. Their ceramic work pulls these methods together, often through the medium of a carefully chosen small factory or studio working to Hinchcliffe and Barber designs. Control over the process leaves the space for the artists to plough more time into the creative thought which keeps the designs fresh.

There is one other defining component in Hinchcliffe and Barber's work: the mission to communicate. Both artists have always been committed to the value of education. They feel strongly indebted to their art-school training, and the way in which they were encouraged to experiment and create across a wide range of mediums. They have never lost that interest in innovation or trial. The teaching programmes that Hinchcliffe and Barber offer at their French studio enable them to inspire vibrancy and enjoyment of craft in their students. It seems only natural that they should wish to continue that communication and share their creative energy through every available medium.

Simon Olding,
Head of Arts and Museums,
Russell-Cotes Art Gallery and Museum,
Bournemouth

INTRODUCTION

❖

OUR ANNOUNCEMENT PLATTER. THIS IS USED AT EXHIBITIONS AND SHOWS.

A FESTIVE PLATTER DECORATED WITH CUT SPONGES.

Ceramic Style is about how we have developed our ideas over the last ten years. Our style is not amazingly sophisticated or avant-garde. It belongs to a friendly, English popular art tradition. Hopefully, it steers a path between the extremes and constraints of studio and art pottery, on the one hand, and mass-produced pottery on the other.

When we started, we knew what we wanted to achieve, but the difficulty was in knowing where to begin. Pottery is a vast and sometimes complex craft, which encompasses many skills, much like any discipline, even cooking, gardening and knitting. The secret of success, we decided, was setting limitations, deciding specifically what to make and initially learning only what we needed to know to produce the ceramic pieces we wanted. As we became more experienced, we were able to consider branching out into other directions. We started by developing plates and platters, because these flat shapes can easily be made and provide an ideal surface for decoration. We then chose a glaze that would give us brilliant colours.

When learning a craft it is vitally important to gain a good knowledge of materials and methods, and it is very interesting and satisfying to develop new skills, but for us it is only a means to an end, a way of turning our ideas into a tangible form. It is all too easy to get so immersed in the techniques that you lose sight of what you are trying to achieve. We hope our approach avoids this. It can be distressing to see a good idea poorly executed, but equally so to see good craftsmanship misdirected.

WE QUITE OFTEN DESIGN IN THE DINING ROOM WHERE IT IS WARMER
THAN THE STUDIOS. THE DRESSER AND ARTISTS' MATERIALS.

11

SPONGED MUGS, HAND-PAINTED PLATTERS, WHITE FLOWER PLATES AND
A VINE-LEAF BOWL ARE MIXED IN WITH OUR COLLECTION OF TRADITIONAL
BLUE-AND-WHITE POTTERY. THE LOWER SHELF OF THE DRESSER SHOWS
SOME OF OUR COUNTRY POTTERY. THIS PICTURE WAS TAKEN IN 1985.

It is particularly satisfying using pottery that you have made and decorated yourself. Pottery that is so familiar is like an extension of oneself. We consider ourselves very fortunate to use every day the shapes that we have developed. We find them generous and pleasing. An early dresser picture shows our handmade sponge-ware with some old and traditional blue-and-white pottery that we have collected over the years.

A more recent picture of the dresser shows the same blue-and-white sponging and some plain blue – our vine leaf and tessera tulip. These are our favourite everyday shapes, colours and patterns. The blue-and-white range that we developed for the British retail group, Next, perfectly complement these original pieces.

We use our blue-and-white animal design, Dorset Delft, in our kitchen. The complementary fabric and tiles combine simplicity, interest and pattern. This is a look that we particularly like. All our pieces mix beautifully together, so that any combination of our pottery takes care of our needs for the everyday serving of food and entertaining both practically and aesthetically.

We derive much satisfaction and fun from the addition of a festive plate for a special meal or occasion. The subject matter and colour of each dresser plate is chosen to enhance the presentation of a meal.

Vast quantities of pottery are not needed if you use this system of basic colour with occasional festive platters. We have become very familiar with the patterns and how different meals will look on each design. For example, black grapes look stunning on our steeplechase plate, and the vine leaf is nearly always used to present the orange cake.

Amongst our recipe books we have an old copy of *Mrs Beeton's Household Management.*

A WHITE FLOWER PLATE.

CROISSANTS AND BREAD ARE KEPT WARM ON A TRADITIONAL RANGE.

Sunday lunch served on a white flower platter ready to be carried out to the dining table.

What is striking in the lovely illustrations is the importance and care given to the presentation of meals and the harmony between the food and plate or setting. Many sets of china were required to achieve this richness and variety, although Mrs Beeton mentions that 'simplicity' is to be aimed for. Simplicity in her terms, and at her time, now seems very elaborate indeed.

Simplicity was not always the aim. In the early eighteenth century, lavish table decorations were often made from sugar confectionery or wax. Later, when porcelain had been developed and decorations became permanent, a great deal of time and skill was spent on these centre pieces. Sometimes whole scenes were created, such as meadows or seascapes – subject matter that we often draw upon. Great realism was achieved, but this fashion for fantasy declined with the classical revival.

We were once commissioned to make a complete dinner service for a horse-loving friend. We developed a variation of our steeplechase design, and the result was so satisfying that we were inspired to make another set. This was then carted off to a local point-to-point, packed in a traditional wicker basket, and we persuaded a friend to devise and cook a suitable menu. The day was memorable, not only for the biting cold, but for the pleasing and delicious result of all our effort. We attracted a lot of interest whilst arranging game pies, salads and desserts on the plates.

The simple addition of a festive plate or plates to the existing daily pottery, or platters, offered to friends and family on special occasions, provides a conversation piece for guests and nostalgia for the owner. We have made vine-leaf plates for vineyard owners and train platters for railway enthusiasts, among many other designs.

GOOSEBERRY TART ON A YELLOW TULIP PLATE CREATING A SUMMER LOOK.

TOP: TURKISH ORANGE CAKE AND RASPBERRIES ON A COLLECTION OF SPONGED AND VINE-LEAF POTTERY.

The steeplechase china in use at a point-to-point meeting in Dorset.

The three sizes of platter nestle snugly into one another.

Every family has special occasions to celebrate. For a daughter's wedding we used our yellow tulip platters and vases. These looked very fresh and pretty – the simple design enhanced the flowers and food and was not overpowering. The bridal bouquet contained the bride's favourite flower, honeysuckle, so we painted a large honeysuckle dresser plate for future use. This was dated and personalised on the back.

We have developed three sizes of platter – more rectangular than oval in form – and also three sizes of oval platter used mainly to carry our fish designs. These shapes really come into their own when serving a buffet. We chose simplicity using one colour only for the yellow tulip wedding platters, but we have sometimes used a rich mixture of colour and pattern on our platters to great effect.

We have a lot of fun with Christmas designs. There is an endless variety of imagery associated with Christmas and mid-winter festivals. All the effort that you have put into designing your motif really comes into its own at this time of year. The stencils can be used to make cards or

16

even as a template for cutting marzipan decorations for the cake for instance.

Hand-painted turkey platters are used for serving the main course of our Christmas dinner, and there is the added excitement that these plates are only displayed and used for the twelve days of Christmas. We have always thought it a

17

DORSET DELFT IS THE NAME WE HAVE GIVEN TO OUR FARMYARD
RANGE IN BLUE AND WHITE IN USE IN OUR KITCHEN.

very glamorous idea to have a complete set of Christmas china. We have not achieved this yet, but we have made a Christmas-cake plate and teaplates in our favourite Christmas pattern.

Besides using decorative plates for the presentation of food, plates, tiles and platters can also be displayed on walls, on hangers, on shelves and on plate stands. The illustrations in this book will show you how we use them and give you some ideas. We often hang our cockerel plates in nooks and crannies. The image is very traditional in Normandy, where we spend a lot of our time – there is a cockerel weather vane on almost every church steeple, and there are also numerous folklore stories concerning cockerels. The cockerel keeps cropping up on our plates and the image is constantly evolving.

A look around the ceramic collections in museums reveals a wealth of purely decorative plates. These often reflect the passions of the artist or the commissioner.

Hand-painters may consider painting portrait plates. We love the idea of these, but it is just as pleasing to name and date the plate in order to personalise it. We did this for a children's birthday party. Each child's place was laid at the table with a named plate bearing an animal, and these were taken home at the end of the party.

In this book we hope that, by showing how we apply our design ideas to ceramics, we will inspire you to create objects and perhaps even complete environments from your own ideas. The stencils that we show you how to develop and use can be applied directly on to paper, walls, fabric or indeed anything else that you can make work. Though we have concentrated here on exploring some of the possibilities of pottery decoration, there is no reason to confine your ideas to ceramics any more than we do.

HOMEMADE MINCE PIES AND A CHRISTMAS PUDDING SIT COMFORTABLY ON OUR HOLLY-BORDERED PLATES AMONGST THE SEASONAL MISTLETOE AND HOLLY.

A COLLECTION OF FISH PLATES HANGING ON THE WALL OF OUR NORMANDY FARMHOUSE.

A COCKEREL PLATE HANGING INSIDE A TRADITIONAL STONE FIREPLACE.

A PEEP AT A COCKEREL PLATE SEEN AT SUNDOWN IN THE BREAD OVEN.

PINK COCKEREL PLATES STORED READY FOR USE ON A SHELF ABOVE
THE WOOD-FIRED BREAD OVEN.

TOP: FARM AND FIELD ANIMALS AND BIRDS DECORATE THESE PLATES
WHICH ARE SIMILAR TO THOSE WE USE FOR NAMED CHILDREN'S PLATES.

21

STARTING IN
CERAMICS

❖

Both of us were trained in the arts. John completed his training at the Royal College of Art in London and Wendy studied painting at the Slade, the art department of University College, London. As students we were encouraged to experiment with and explore every conceivable method and technique in order to express our ideas to their best advantage. We have continued to work in this way as the photographs and our themes show.

In the 1960s when we first started thinking about ceramics, we were both hand-weaving large decorative pieces, which were very strong on colour, pattern and surface texture. John was weaving large rugs which used masses of rags or cloth carefully dyed to meet his requirements, while Wendy was weaving tapestries with landscape and garden themes. However, hand-weaving can be a very slow activity – the period between conceiving the idea and finally realising it was sometimes very long indeed. This meant that we were frustrated by having

BLUE-AND-WHITE POTTERY IN GLOUCESTERSHIRE.

A TAPESTRY WOVEN BY WENDY BARBER. THE COLOUR IS BUILT UP BY TWISTING MANY DIFFERENT YARNS TOGETHER TO FORM THE WEFT. THE GARDEN IS AT ATHELHAMPTON IN DORSET AND SHOWS A FOUNTAIN SEEN THROUGH THE YEW TOPIARY HEDGES.

far more ideas than we could possibly produce by such a slow method.

The late 1960s and early 1970s saw a tremendous surge of creative energy in all areas of the crafts. The Crafts Council had just been formed and the Victoria and Albert Museum held its highly successful exhibition, 'The Craftsman's Art', showing a comprehensive collection of all types of crafts – ceramics, textiles, weaving, glass and so on. It became very fashionable to be an 'artist craftsman' and the name rightly acknowledged those craftsmen whose work involved design, decoration and art. Traditional activities such as weaving saw amazing changes – different materials such as rope were used and three-dimensional and sculptural tapestries began to appear. Jewellers were experimenting with materials as diverse as nylon, aluminium or plastics, pottery was becoming ceramic sculpture and rugs were looking better hung on walls than on floors.

We had always been interested by one of the principles of the fashion industry, whereby the 'one-off' designer couture collections influenced and directed a far larger manufactured 'off the peg' garment industry. The designer's role was to take the risks that a factory couldn't afford and create an interest that the factories would pick up and produce on a large scale. This appealed to us, and though not trained in ceramics, which was the area we believed would offer the most potential for our ideas, we set up our studio and began evolving a distinctive ceramic style.

We started by reading every relevant book that we could lay our hands on. We travelled as much as we could, looking not only in the museums, but also in hardware stores and department stores. We sought technical advice from experts and knowledgeable friends. In the very early days, we had some difficulty with the chemistry, but quickly found that the suppliers of the raw materials were willing to help. Then we researched decorating techniques on the pottery that we were attracted to.

We had strong ideas in our heads about what we were aiming for and searched for a way to realise them. The forms that we began to produce had a Mediterranean feel. To help us refine them we would draw them or throw them. After a lot of experiments we eventually decided on a few shapes that seemed to have the character we were after and were suitable for the sorts of decorations that we knew we were going to develop. As we familiarized ourselves with our new shapes and became used to the techniques, we were able to consider experimenting with different forms of

A SELECTION OF SIMPLE DOMESTIC COUNTRY POTTERY, BOTH OLD AND NEW, FROM OUR OWN COLLECTION ARRANGED IN ONE OF OUR STONE OUTBUILDINGS.

decoration. In the early days as many of the plates were painted as were sponged. As you will see from our projects in Chapter 6, we have now developed a combination of the two.

We were greatly influenced by the strong images – fishes and octopuses and so on – that we saw in Crete, not only in the ancient potteries in museums but also in the peasant pottery we saw around us. Shortly after that, John collaborated with Janice Tchalenco, a stoneware potter who was experimenting with decorative effects on pottery. This collaboration culminated in an exhibition of platters and bowls in the Victoria and Albert Museum craft shop. The style of these stoneware pieces varied considerably from the style that Janice had previously developed and for which she is well known. Janice's strength was in the shapes and forms, while John was largely responsible for the methods and style of decoration, and his input into these pieces clearly showed the beginning of our new look. However, stoneware decoration is by nature quite clumsy and blurred, and by this time we had discovered that the decorative quality we were after – quite detailed and more delicate colours – was going to be more easily obtainable if we used earthenware and a majolica glaze.

In 1983, Hinchcliffe and Barber

showed their first platters at the Salisbury Festival. Our hunch that there was a market for colourful, decorative pieces was right. The platters sold well and seemed to please our customers as much as us. Our style was not yet fully developed, but we were getting some of the finer qualities we were aiming for and, satisfied with this first showing of our ideas, determined to pursue and refine them.

In the early 1970s, the artist craftsmen movement had been confined to art schools, but by the early 80s there was a surge in the number of people doing crafts and a growth in interest. Lady Powell started her Chelsea Crafts Fair in the Chelsea Town Hall in London; suddenly the artist craftsman seemed to have a customer who had been primed by features in magazines such as *Country Living*. This was an exciting new movement, and we enjoyed and benefited from it, but we were looking towards industry to develop what we had learned on a larger scale. We had learned the craft not just to make one-off pieces, but to make what we considered to be good, user-friendly designs that could be mass-produced and widely available. London store buyers were by now taking our studio pieces – our 'different' shapes and brighter colours.

By the mid-80s we were unable to

OUR SHAPES DECORATED IN BLUE AND IN WHITE WITH A BLUE RIM. PHOTOGRAPHED IN GLOUCESTERSHIRE.

THESE TWO JUGS WERE PURCHASED IN
TUSCANY, IN THE HILLTOP TOWN OF
CORTONA, AND ARE VERY TYPICAL OF A TYPE
OF WARE PRODUCED IN THE TOWN. COPPER
AND MANGANESE OXIDE ARE SPLASHED ON TO
THE SIDES TO CREATE A SIMPLE BUT EFFECTIVE
DECORATION.

keep up with the orders, so we moved the pottery out of the garage and the glaze area out of what was the dining room – we had spent a lot of time running backwards and forwards with glazed and decorated plates carefully protected from the rain under an umbrella – and set up a small studio in a purpose-built building. We employed assistants that we trained ourselves in our methods and kept vigorous control over the designs. The stencils were always cut by us.

Soon we were selling our designs to factories, which meant that Hinchcliffe and Barber studio ware was much more available. We were able to sell it to Japan, Australia, America and Europe and even keep up with our orders. After a time, however, although the demand was encouraging, we needed to assess the situation. As we continued to expand we were, to all intents and purposes, running not a studio but a mini-factory. This is not what we had set out to do. We decided to disband the studio, where we had to watch over quantities of individual pieces being made by our helpers, and concentrate on ceramics made either by us, individually, or in the factory in large numbers.

Working in this way gives us time to develop our new ideas and also to experiment with new techniques. We

have a small gallery in order to gauge an initial reaction to our ideas, and are privileged enough also to design for industry. Perhaps what we have learned is that there was not an industrial revolution for nothing! Mass-production technology affords us more time to develop an idea, and the pleasure of making pottery by hand in studio conditions.

We hope that the hand-making techniques we show you in this book will help you realise and develop your own ideas.

LARGE OVAL STONEWARE PLATTER WHICH JOHN HINCHCLIFFE DECORATED IN COLLABORATION WITH JANICE TCHALENCO FOR THE VICTORIA AND ALBERT EXHIBITION. THE PLATTER IS SHOWN WITH ITS SUPPORTING ARTWORK.

INSPIRATION
& INFLUENCES

❖

People, places, words, colours, objects, sounds and occasions: all are potentially inspirational, filling your senses and inspiring you to make something.

Watching someone weaving, spinning, painting or throwing a pot can inspire you to try it. Simply handling a material like wool, stone or clay can give you ideas about colour, texture, shape and pattern. Different people respond in totally different ways to all sounds and colours. The problem is directing that response into something tangible without getting bogged down in practicalities and techniques. The obvious solution is to put your ideas and images down on paper – draw them or paint them – not worrying who might look at them or whether or not they are good enough, or whether they conform, and go from there.

Undoubtedly we are influenced and inspired in many different ways. There are many specific objects, places and colours that we are particularly inspired

SHELLS, SEAWEED AND CRABS SURROUND THE
WORKING DRAWINGS AND INITIAL IDEAS FOR A
SEAWEED BORDER FOR A LARGE TILE PANEL.

A COLOURFUL COLLECTION OF FRUIT,
VEGETABLES AND FLOWERS.

by and we describe some of them in detail in Chapter Six. There are also less tangible immediate influences that are tied up with our attitude towards our work generally and what it is we are trying to achieve.

There are particular painters, styles and movements we are drawn to because of their philosophy, energy and vitality, such as Picasso and Hockney who have notably experimented with and explored many other crafts besides painting. We also admire the ideology behind the Omega Workshops that were set up in the early part of this century. This group of people, mainly writers and painters not actively involved in any area of the crafts, produced all kinds of unusually decorative and colourful objects as a direct reaction to the stifling nature of Edwardian society, paintings and decorative arts. We admire the light and assured pieces they produced and their exuberant approach to decoration, which extended over almost every surface that they could find.

There were groups of artists similarly involved in a design reappraisal all over Europe. At about this time, for instance, there was a very interesting phenomenon taking place in France. The Paris couturier Paul Poiret had set up a unique studio called the Atelier Martine where all the designers were young girls, none of them more than fifteen years old. Poiret was interested in the ability of children to produce ideas spontaneously, free from any kind of restraint, and wanted to harness this ability to the design, initially, of fabrics. So successful was the venture that he eventually set up an interior design business where all kinds of other objects were produced. He would take the girls to see things that would stimulate and inspire them – zoos, markets, the seaside, even textile and pottery factories – and then he would leave them to produce their ideas. What he valued was unadulterated ideas and original thinking, an approach we have much sympathy with.

The French painter Dufy was another versatile artist who designed tapestries, clothes, wood engravings, collages and textiles. His stylish and fresh approach to each of these projects is wonderful. Picasso, too, worked on tile panels and other ceramics using many techniques. His series of platters with black decoration on ochre earthenware is reminiscent of the magnificent Greek vases that are to be seen in museums – his bullfighting scenes are as lively and exciting as those the Greeks depicted on their red figure vases of the archaic period. We are drawn not only to the strong stark images he produced but also to his use of 'everyday' scenes. Artists

A SELECTION OF SEASHORE PHOTOGRAPHS.

seem to benefit from a freedom of expression and convention that eludes some crafts people, for whom technique can play too big a part. It is certainly interesting that in Britain at least, far more painters have produced ceramics for industry than potters have, even more so because mass-production supposedly imposes even more constraints on individual freedom of expression than practising a craft in a studio does.

The 1930s in England was a particularly interesting period – painters were involved with every aspect of what could crudely be called 'commercial art'. Every conceivable article from wallpapers and book jackets to textiles and pottery was being designed, if not produced, by painters. Whether it was the *Shell Guide to Dorset*, photographed by Paul Nash and John Piper, or the Harrods 'Modern Art for the Table' exhibition in 1933 which included the work of painters like Ben Nicholson, Graham Sutherland, Eric Ravilious and Duncan Grant, objects went beyond being mere utilitarian artefacts and became inspirational in themselves.

All these approaches have something in common which is very important to us – originality and spontaneity. These elements play a big part in our attitude to our work, but there are also certain traditions that have had an influence on our work, and led us to the use, particularly, of majolica.

MAJOLICA

❖

Majolica essentially refers to the technique of decorating on to an opaque glaze. Although a general term, it tends to refer to Italian work, probably because during the fifteenth century Italy became the centre of trade for this brightly coloured pottery from Spain known as maiolica. The same technique is called faience in France, which most likely derives from the name of the Italian town, Faenza, one of the most influential centres of majolica production. Delft is another term for majolica, and undoubtedly refers to the town of Delft in the Netherlands, where a particularly characteristic style was produced – predominately blue.

Many museums have wonderful collections of panels, dishes, drug pots and plates painted and decorated by hand with almost unbelievable skill and detail. Every conceivable subject, from Biblical scenes and landscapes to copies of engravings and paintings, was lavishly portrayed. This strong pictorial style developed in one direction into what is called 'istoriato', a style so grand it could almost *only* be hung in palaces.

In Italy one can still see majolica being produced at Deruta, but really only as a tourist industry. Holland produces delft tiles as it has done for hundreds of years, but the tradition has hardly changed – the style has nothing modern about it. For a time majolica flourished in the form of peasant or regional pottery, and there are wonderful examples from France, Spain, Germany or Romania, but sadly now, since techniques have advanced and majolica is no longer considered a mainstream form of decoration, these are mostly in museums.

SHALLOW DISH, MAJOLICA ITALIAN
(MONTELUPA).

TOP: HAND-PAINTED BLUE-AND-WHITE
BIRD TILE.

THESE EXAMPLES OF EARLY MAJOLICA FROM THE
RUSSELL-COTES MUSEUM IN BOURNEMOUTH SHOW A
HIGH LEVEL OF EXPERTISE. WE USE THE TRADITIONAL
THEMES SHOWN HERE IN OUR WORK.

ABOVE: ITALIAN MAJOLICA PLATE (CASTELLI) PAINTED
BY AURELIO GRUE, LATE SEVENTEENTH CENTURY.

LEFT: TIN-GLAZED EARTHENWARE TILES (ROTTERDAM
OR GOUDA), SEVENTEENTH CENTURY.

Decorating majolica in a traditional small workshop in Seville, Spain.

Majolica dish.

39

A CORNER OF THE DINING ROOM.

OUR FISH PLATTER TOGETHER WITH A FISH
FABRIC WE HAVE PRINTED WITH WAX TO RESIST
THE INDIGO DYE.

ENGLISH BLUE-AND-WHITE POTTERY

No other colour has had quite the same impact on ceramic decoration as blue. The blues in ceramics come from cobalt oxide, which produces a wide range of extremely beautiful and strong colours that are reliable and easily applied.

It was not until the introduction of opaque glazes that cobalt came into its own, but when majolica painting was introduced, its virtues were quickly realized. It is always the dominant colour in majolica decoration, and in many examples of Dutch and English delft it is often the only colour used.

It is not surprising that a strong blue and white fashion began to develop. In part, it evolved from the comparative ease by which blue could be applied. Spongeware is a good example of the combination of pottery that was essentially utilitarian and quick to make and a simple method of decoration that became synonymous with the country. Vast quantities of this ware were shipped to the settlers of North America and Canada during the nineteenth century from English and Scottish potteries. It is not surprising, since it was neither costly nor complicated to make, that blue spongeware of every type was such a prominent feature of early American homesteads.

Cottage Pottery, as it is sometimes called, involved decorating on a principle similar to that of rubber stamping or potato printing. Sometimes fine sponges were used simply to dab oxide on the ware; more often simple designs were cut into them. This technique was often used in conjunction with some hand-painting. Interestingly, because many country people used only bowls for eating their meals, they were by far the most decorated item. Although blue was the predominant colour, this form of spongeware can be extremely colourful, and wonderful examples survive of rose, sunflower and tulip designs. However, because spongeware was so utilitarian and was never considered a mainstream form of ceramic decoration, few English museums have good collections. The Stoke-on-Trent City Museum is one of the few places where there is a particularly wonderful showcase full of sponged cow creamers.

The arrival and development of transfer printing in the 1750s consolidated the popularity of blue and white. Alongside the perfection of white clay bodies and glazes, this new method revolutionized pottery decoration. The ease with which images could now be reproduced meant, suddenly, that decorated pottery became accessible to many more sections of society and that the subject matter would become wider and more variable. Everything and anything was included and, as the process was perfected, all manner of items, including tiles, were decorated.

What contributed most to the success of blue-and-white earthenware, and plates in particular, was the way in which such a useful object could be displayed like a picture or print. Certainly, at a time when many people could not read or write and newspapers were not generally available, what better way could there be of portraying something of major interest – a coronation, a horserace, a sea battle or a

A COLLECTION OF HAND-PAINTED BIRD PLATES IN BLUE AND WHITE.

OUR COW PLATES AND WARE CREATE A STRONG BLUE-AND-WHITE LOOK.

41

romantic landscape. However, our favourites are the floral plates. In fact the theme plates often had floral borders, and floral decoration was a very strong theme throughout.

Floral borders are often derivative of wallpaper patterns. These borders proved very popular and are still around today, used in modern interpretations of traditional designs. Distinctive borders were designed to go with each dinner service, regardless of whether the wares carried a single pattern or a variety of patterns. This is an interesting design device, because it unifies lots of different images into a set. Examples of these borders can be found if you search for English blue and white transferred designs dating from the eighteenth century. Borders might be separated from the main pattern or image on the plates by a line or a smaller sub-border. For example, in a landscape plate, trees or branches might be used to form a view, thus giving the scene a sense of perspective. Plates using this decorative device were known as 'Grotto border plates'.

Floral designs are very popular, and some very beautiful plates exist whose designs are taken from botanical illustrations. Amongst these are the Wedgwood series of botanical plates introduced in 1810, which reflected John Wedgwood's horticultural interests and whose designs were adapted from William Curtis's botanical magazine. The flowers are well placed on the plate, and the border is simple but effective – we find this series very pleasing. Our particular interest in these sorts of plates is in the fact that they are both functional and decorative. It pleases us that they look nice just sitting on a dresser. We also love the riches that can be achieved with a subdued palette. These things have had quite an influence on our styles.

A SELECTION OF OUR BLUE-AND-WHITE POTTERY ON A STRIPPED PINE DRESSER.

RAW
MATERIALS

❖

The availability and technical refinement that has gone into ceramic equipment and materials means that it has become quite a straight-forward craft. There are clays, glazes, kilns and colours to fulfil almost every requirement. The equipment required to make plates and tiles is not difficult to obtain or even very expensive. Do not be tempted to buy more than you need to carry out your project. If you get really involved in the techniques of pottery and begin to explore other methods, you can always buy more equipment later.

The technical aspect of pottery – the firing and glazing – is pure chemistry. Clay and glazes are formulated to perform specific tasks, they change drastically when they are fired to high temperatures. If you get the chemistry or the firing conditions wrong, your ceramic piece simply will not work. However, because clay and glaze bodies are so carefully formulated, the possibility of failure is greatly diminished.

A RICH AND COLOURFUL COMBINATION OF FLOWERS, POTTERY AND INDIGO TULIP FABRIC.

A SELECTION OF MATERIALS:
BAG OF CLAY, RUBBER KIDNEY PALETTES,
CHEESEWIRE FOR CUTTING CLAY, SIEVES,
APRON, MEASURING JUG, PLASTIC BUCKETS,
SPONGES, ROLLING PIN, KILN GLOVES.

CLAY

Clay is formed by the decomposition over thousands of years of feldspathic rock, of which granite is an example. The mineral feldspar is used in many glazes and most clays. As the feldspar decomposes and is broken up by geologic weathering, other elements are washed away leaving alumina and silica. All the different kinds of feldspar contain these two essential elements which, after long exposure to moisture, become hydrated or chemically combined with water, resulting in pure clay. Pure clay, called kaolin (or china clay) is very rare and only occurs naturally. This is called primary clay. It is coarse in texture, non-plastic and difficult to work with in that it is highly refractory and resists heat. It is usually mixed with other materials and is an essential ingredient, for instance, in the manufacture of porcelain. The main sources of china clay in Europe are Limoges, Meissen, Halle and the Ukraine. It can also be found in Devonshire and Cornwall.

Most clays are impure – through erosion and weathering they are washed away into streams and rivers and gather impurities on the way. In this process they become finer and their nature changes. These clays are called secondary clays. There is a huge variety, some stoneware and some earthenware; it is the variety of their components and the types of impurities that make them behave so differently.

We are concerned here with earthenware clays, which are usually red, buff or white and are fired at a comparatively low temperature of 1050 to 1150°C (1922-2102°F). They are porous when fired. Stoneware clays become vitreous when fired, and the temperature range is generally higher – between 1200 and 1300°C (2192-2372°F).

Many products like bricks and tiles are made

with clay straight from the ground. However, most clays are carefully prepared blends of different materials. These blends are called bodies. Most suppliers list at least a dozen clay bodies in red or white clays, and they are usually available in 10 to 25 kg bags. Ask your supplier for advice about which clays to use.

GLAZE

Glazing, as the name suggests, covers the surface of the ware with a thin film of glass. This, after firing, will improve the appearance and durability of the piece and make it impervious to liquids. Glass is really melted sand or silica (ground flint or quartz), which on its own is not sufficient to glaze a pot or plate since it does not melt at the temperatures most pottery kilns are fired to. For this reason fluxes are added – they lower the melting point of the silica. If you were to use silica and flux alone, however, they would make a glaze so liquid that during firing it would run off the pottery; therefore, a third ingredient, alumina (from clay, chinastone and feldspar), is added to give the glaze viscosity – this makes the glaze adhere to the pot when fired.

The fluxes come from many different sources – each has a different fluxing, or temperature-lowering, strength and will affect the surface quality of the glaze differently. Many glazes are in fact named or classified according to the kind of flux that has been used in its composition. In ceramics the flux is usually an oxide, often lead, potassium, sodium, zinc, boric, magnesium, barium or calcium oxide.

A glaze can be soft, hard, clear, opaque, gloss, matt, raw, fritted lead, leadless alkaline, stoneware or earthenware. The considerations that govern its use and application are far from

A SELECTION OF TILE CUTTERS RESTING ON A SLAB ROLLER WHICH CAN BE USED INSTEAD OF A ROLLING PIN FOR ROLLING OUT SLABS OF CLAY.

being arbitrary – when you have selected the type of glaze you require, you must make sure that there is a compatibility between the clay body, the glaze and the firing temperature. Your supplier will advise you about this. We purchase our glaze ready-mixed to our exact requirements.

When glazing, do ensure that your 'biscuit' – or fired clay body – is clean, that the glaze has been mixed and applied correctly and that the biscuit has been fired to the correct temperature check with your supplier.

We use an earthenware body and a majolica glaze. This opaque glaze totally covers the fired biscuit.

Tin oxide has always been the traditional material in making a glaze opaque; however, zirconium oxide, zinc oxide and titanium oxide also perform the same function and each will alter the surface quality and whiteness of the fired glaze.

ONCE YOU HAVE DECIDED ON YOUR GLAZE, IT IS USEFUL TO MAKE A SAMPLE PLATE TO SHOW HOW THE STAINS AND OXIDES WILL LOOK WHEN FIRED.

COLOUR: OXIDES AND STAINS

Traditionally, certain metal oxides are used to colour ceramics. Although insoluble in water, they disperse in it as a powder, and are painted on to the unfired glaze surface. When fired they then melt and fuse with the glaze. Although there are a lot of different oxides, probably the most useful are cobalt for blues, copper for greens, iron for red, browns and manganese for purples and browns. Some of these look very different, when painted on, from the colour they will be after firing.

The most useful, and in fact the only oxide we use, is cobalt oxide, which gives a wonderful range of ceramic blues. This, probably more than any other, is the essential majolica colour.

Apart from cobalt oxide we also use glaze stains which are highly refined, manufactured oxides which we find extremely reliable and easy to use. Like the oxides, they are powders that disperse in water and can be applied very easily by brush or sponge. Bear in mind that *all* of these powders are poisonous.

KILNS

Although kilns can be heated by wood, oil or gas, we use electric kilns, which are the most common these days. Ask your supplier for advice.

IF YOU HAVEN'T GOT A KILN

If you do not have access to a kiln, all the design ideas talked about here can be tried out on self-hardening clay that was developed for use in schools and does not require firing. This clay is available from most major craft suppliers, and is called 'Real Clay' Air Hardening.

A range of colours has been developed to match this clay (they can also be used for any other porous surface, including wood or paper). These products are for decorative purposes only.

TWO TOP-LOADING AND ONE FRONT-LOADING ELECTRIC KILN. ALL ARE IDEAL FOR SCHOOLS, DOMESTIC AND LIGHT INDUSTRIAL USE. FULL SPECIFICATIONS CAN BE OBTAINED FROM OUR MAIN UK SUPPLIER LISTED AT THE BACK OF THIS BOOK.

MAKING PLATES & TILES

❖

Plates, shallow dishes and tiles are simple to make; no specialized skills are required. Clay is either rolled out into sheets and layed over plate moulds or pressed into tile moulds. Hollow shapes are either thrown by hand on a wheel or cast in moulds using liquid clay.

We use hump moulds made of plaster of Paris for making plates, and shallow wooden moulds for making tiles. The principle for both is the same. Plastic clay which has been pressed on to or into a mould will form the shape of the surfaces it has come into contact with and retain it when it has dried.

Although sometimes considered a rather impersonal method of making shapes, the use of moulds suits our requirements exactly because the form, once chosen, remains the same and enables us to concentrate on the decoration.

A COLLECTION OF COCKERELS AND HENS.

THE TEMPLATE IS SCRAPED AROUND THE PLATE
TO FORM THE PROFILE.

MAKING A MOULD

MIXING PLASTER OF PARIS

Plaster of paris is made from gypsum. Gypsum is a hard rock when it is mined, but when heated it is reduced to a true white powder. This is how we buy our plaster of Paris. When it is remixed with water it sets into a hard, solid mass within about fifteen minutes. You should always store it carefully – keep it dry and take care never to get it anywhere near clay that is going to be used and fired. Plaster in clay causes it to explode when firing. When you are cleaning up after using plaster of Paris, take care not to put any down the drain because it will block it up due to the speed at which it sets. Leave any surplus to set in the container you mixed it in and then crack it up and put it in the bin. Plaster should be mixed in the proportion of three parts plaster to two parts water or 1.7kg plaster to 710ml water. You will find you will be able to gauge the correct consistency with practice. Plaster of Paris should always be added to water, not the reverse.

We use a washing-up bowl kept for the purpose of mixing plaster of Paris, but any plastic container will do. We half fill the bowl with water and slowly sprinkle handfuls of plaster on to the surface. When small islands of plaster stand above the water level, you have probably added enough. To mix, slip your hand into the water and very gently agitate it below the surface to mix the two together, being extremely careful to avoid making any air bubbles.

You must use the mixed plaster immediately to make the mould. You will notice that the plaster starts to warm up as it hardens; it starts to harden in the first ten minutes, but the whole process takes several days.

Plaster of Paris poured on to soft clay or clean glass will not stick, but it will stick fast on most other surfaces, particularly other plaster. In order to avoid sticking, you must 'size' the surface to be moulded to make sure it is no longer absorbent. Use a commercially available mould-maker's size, or alternatively apply several coats of vaseline, olive oil or soft soap.

SIZE AND SHAPE

In order to help you decide on the size and the shape of the plate or platter you want to make, we advise you to have a good look at the plates you have around you. We suggest you begin with a very simple shape – one without too much of a rim that is not too deep. You should think about the cross-section of your plate – you will need to decide whether or not to have sharp or soft curves, and how gently or steeply the border slopes into the middle. Once you have taken these decisions, it is a good idea to make a drawing, and perhaps a model, before make your mould.

HUMP MOULDS

To make our plates and platters, we use hump moulds. A sheet of flattened clay (about ³/₈ inch or 8mm thick) is placed on to the mould, which impresses the inside surface of the clay with the form of the plate.

There are several ways of making a hump mould – we describe two methods here. The first involves making a hollow mould from which you can then make a hump mould, and the second involves making the hump mould in one step.

MAKING A HOLLOW MOULD

Take a sheet of hardboard 3-4 inches (75-100mm) larger than the model from which you are working. Make sure there is a good area of board around the model. Now draw on to the hardboard the outside outline of the plate. Alternatively, you can cut another piece of hardboard, cardboard or paper to shape so that it gives the outline, and tack it on to the bottom layer of the hardboard. On to this surface, and within the outline, build up the shape of the inside of the plate in reverse, with soft clay. Leave it to harden slightly so that you can smooth the surface with a rubber kidney and fine, wet sponges. The model is now ready to be prepared for casting.

CASTING THE HOLLOW MOULD

You now need to build a 'cottle' or wall to contain the plaster when it is poured on to the model. This can be made from stiff card, thin flexible metal sheeting or lino and is built up around the model about half an inch to an inch (10-25mm) away from the outline. It must rise at least 2-3 inches (50-75mm) above the highest point of the model. Stick it to the baseboard with clay to prevent the plaster running out, and keep it in shape by tying string around it. Pour the mixed plaster in and leave it to dry. As it dries, try to make the top surface, which will become the mould's base, as level as possible. A metal ruler or an old surform or file is ideal for smoothening any bumps.

When the plaster of Paris is dry – after about 20 to 30 minutes – carefully separate it from the model. The cavity in the plaster is the hollow mould. The next step is to turn this hollow mould into a hump mould, but you will need to leave it for three or four days until it has properly hardened.

CASTING A HUMP MOULD FROM A HOLLOW MOULD

To cast a hump mould, size the cavity extremely well in order to make sure the inside surface is completely non-absorbent. Then pour in the mixed plaster of Paris.

At the point that the plaster of Paris is beginning to harden, within five minutes or so, insert some wire into the centre section – we use 15 inches (40cm) or so bent into three prongs and surround it with another cottle. Fill this with plaster to cast a small stem or foot. The size of the foot depends on the size of the plate you are making, but it should be at least half as wide as the plate in order to support the mould. Ours are usually about 5 inches (125mm) high.

When all this has set hard, the new hump mould can be removed from the hollow mould. You now have a hump or mushroom mould ready for use. You can use the hollow mould to make as many hump moulds as you need.

Hollow moulds are particularly useful for decorating with slip since the unfired damp clay is supported in the mould.

COMPLETED MOULD OF AN OVAL PLATE SHOWING DRAWING PROFILE AND MODELLING TOOLS.

MAKING A HUMP MOULD

❖

With this method, plaster of Paris is moulded with a template to form the actual shape of the inside of the plate. This process is particularly suited to larger plates.

To try and give a clear and concise visual guide to how a mould is made the photographs were taken in a mould-making studio in Stoke-on-Trent.

A mould can be made in different ways, although the general principles remain relatively the same. These pictures illustrate the principles involved and are relatively self-explanatory.

1 Drawing out the plate shape to the exact size.

2 This template will be used to form the profile of the plate.

3 The plaster plate base is made to the exact size and shape of plate.

4 Ready to begin. Clay and cottle are placed around the plaster shape ready for the plaster to be poured.

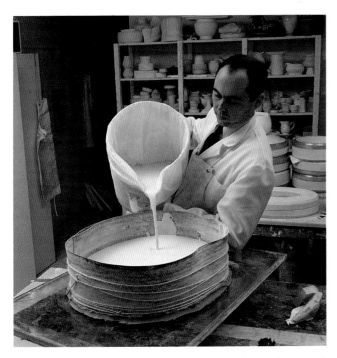

5 *Plaster being poured on to the plaster base with cottle in position.*

6 *The cottle is now removed, revealing new plaster on the base ready for shaping.*

7 *The template is scraped around the plate to form the profile.*

8 *The finished plate is gently smoothed using a rubber kidney.*

MAKING THE TEMPLATE

Draw to scale on paper the cross-section of the plate that you wish to make. Then cut a template of it out of Perspex, wood or thin metal using a fretsaw or other cutting tool. The template should extend beyond the centre of the plate and allow an inch (25mm) or so below the rim to make a definite edge and to give the model a depth also of about an inch (25mm). It is important to cut a piece of hardboard to the outline of the plate so that the template can be drawn around its edge to give the mould a uniform shape. Fix this to a larger piece of board that you have taken great care to size well so that it is impervious.

POURING THE MOULD

Pour some plaster slowly on to the base and as it sets – this happens almost immediately – pour more and more plaster on to it, all the time drawing the template around the edge of the outline. The template should scrape away the plaster of Paris before it sets completely to make the hump mould.

A small template can be used but we prefer larger ones attached to a wooden bridge that extends over the mould and gives a firmer grip as well as holding the template at the correct height.

When your mould is complete, fill any small holes with more plaster and smooth the surface with 'wet or dry' sandpaper and sponges. When it is dry and hard – after two or three days – your hump mould is ready for use.

THIS TILE PANEL WAS COMMISSIONED FOR THE ENTRANCE OF THE
CERAMICS COLLECTION FOR THE SALISBURY MUSEUM. WE HANDMADE
THE TILES AND COVERED THEM WITH A THIN MAJOLICA GLAZE – THEN
WE HAND-PAINTED FAVOURITE PIECES FROM THE MUSEUM'S
COLLECTION.

MAKING A PLATE
FROM YOUR MOULD

1 Rolling out the clay between strips of wood is a good way to control the thickness.

2 The mould is now ready to be covered with the sheet of clay.

3 Place the rolled-out piece of clay gently on to the mould.

4 Gently press the clay on to the contours of the mould with your hands.

5 *Use the rubber kidney to smooth the clay on to the mould.*

6 *Cut off excess clay with a cheesewire. Finally, stroke the plate gently all over with a rubber kidney. The plate can now be left to dry slowly.*

PREPARING THE CLAY

We use the same clay to make both our plates and tiles and recommend the use of prepared clay bodies. Clays vary considerably and most manufactured clay bodies have been engineered to perform specific functions. In this case we would recommend you select a clay suitable for press moulding rather than throwing – ask your supplier for advice.

When clay is exposed to air it dries out, therefore it is essential to keep it stored in an airtight container or wrapped in plastic bags. We keep the clay in its original bags and the trimmings in large airtight bins. This waste clay can be re-used.

Prepared clay is almost perfect to use without any preliminary preparation, but it is essential that it contains no air and is not too dry or too wet. To get the clay into the right condition for use, it is necessary to 'wedge' it.

Do make sure you have a firm, solid table to work on – this is essential. To wedge, take lumps of clay off the main block and bang them smartly together on the table as many as ten or twenty times, regularly cutting them in half with a cheesewire between bangings The purpose of this is to drive the air pockets out of the clay as these will explode during firing.

Kneading is part of the conditioning process. If the clay is slightly wet, the kneading process will help to dry it out – this is made much easier if you knead the clay on an absorbent surface such as wood or canvas-covered board. If the clay is too dry, handling it with wet hands and kneading the moisture into it will remedy the problem.

The kneading process is similar to that of kneading dough for bread making. Do use a firm table. When you have the clay in place, use the palms of both hands and push into the clay away from you. Repeat the process again and again, bringing it back and rolling it towards you and pressing down into the centre of it and pushing it away from you again. It is important that you don't 'fold' any air into it – the aim is to squeeze any air out while improving its condition. Repeat this action, using both palms together, at least a dozen or so times. Gradually the lump will begin to feel ready to use and will form into an ox head shape. Kneading and wedging are soon mastered with practice.

SHAPE THE THROWING 'CLOT' BY ROLLING IT ON THE BENCH.

COVERING
THE MOULD

Covering moulds is not particularly messy; unlike throwing, there is hardly any water involved, and no liquid clay. All our clay preparation is done on a large piece of canvas stretched and stapled over a board approximately 3 feet by 2 feet (90cm by 61cm) which can be attached to a more solid table with cramps or screws. We find we prefer canvas to wood, marble or slate – one of its advantages is that it is easy to clean or replace, and underneath it there is always a clean surface ready.

The only other essential pieces of equipment are a rolling pin, which can be a length of alloy scaffolding tube for larger areas (available from a builder's merchant), a rubber kidney and a cheesewire for cutting clay.

Our plates are approximately one centimetre thick, and this is achieved by rolling out the clay between two strips of wood one centimetre in depth. The prepared clay is rolled into balls of the weight required comfortably to cover the particular size of your mould – you will have to gauge this by eye. Once you know how much clay you need to cover your mould, you can weigh it so you know accurately how much to use next time. Slap down your ball of clay on to the canvas cloth repeatedly until it is almost flat. Then roll your clay between the strips of wood until the correct thickness is achieved. Like rolling pastry, the clay should be turned and rolled in different directions. As the backcloth becomes impregnated with clay after continual use, it should be scraped with a metal ruler.

Once the clay is the required size and depth

to cover your mould, allowing for a generous overlap of up to an inch (2.5cm), smooth the surface with the soft rubber kidney. This smoothed surface will become the inside of the plate, the part that will be in contact with the hump mould.

Now lift this sheet of clay and place it on the mould. Use the kidney gently to smooth the clay into the contours of the mould. Then trim the excess clay with a cheesewire – making sure you hold it firmly, draw it round the edge of the mould.

The drying stage is the most delicate for as the clay dries it will separate from the surface of the mould and begin to distort. After 12 to 24 hours, depending on how warm your work area is, it will have changed from being soft to leather-hard. When your clay plate is solid enough to keep its shape, take it off its mould and place it gently on its face on a newspaper-covered board. If any edge has warped, gently press it back into position.

It is very important that the plate is allowed to dry slowly and evenly, and it should be turned over regularly. Keep an eye on the plate every few hours for any signs of warping, and press gently back into shape. The drying process can take quite a long time – on average a few days, though some of our very large plates take weeks to dry out. For this reason we have several moulds and make our plates in batches. When our studio was in full pro-duction, we made hundreds of different shaped plates a week and developed a system of firing and decorating that gave us plenty of bone-dry plates which we biscuit-fired and stacked. This ensured that we never ran out of our essential raw material – plates and platters for decoration. Once the plate is bone dry it is ready for its first firing.

A CHEESEWIRE IS USED TO CUT EXCESS CLAY FROM THE EDGE OF THE MOULD.

MAKING TILES

Although there are many methods of making handmade tiles we have chosen to illustrate the method generally used by us but photographed in a small traditional brick and tile company in Derbyshire. These pictures convey far better than words the principle of tile making.

The preliminary stages in preparing the clay for making tiles are the same as for plates. You must wedge and knead it to expel any pockets of air and to get the clay into a workable state.

The simplest way to make a tile is by laying a square card template, cut to the required size, over a flattened slab of clay. The clay is then cut with a knife or sharp needle following the edge of the template. You can produce a perfectly adequate tile using this technique. There are, however, more efficient methods – tile cutters are one. These are pressed into a large

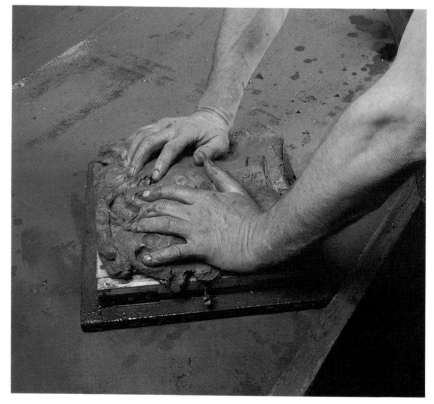

1 The mould is cleaned and prepared with oil and a brush.

2 Press the 'clot' into the wooden frame, having dusted the false base.

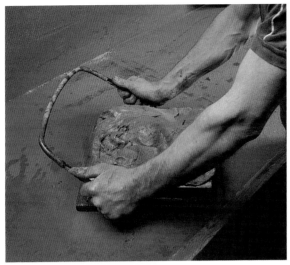

3 Remove excess clay from the tile frame. The easiest way to do this is to cut off the top of the 'clot' with a wire bow.

sheet of clay and an ejection plate pushes out the tile. If you have a large quantity of tiles to make, it is worth investing in one of these, but bear in mind that only small tiles – up to about 4 inches (10cm) – can be made by this method. They can be purchased from most pottery suppliers.

One of the advantages of handmade tiles is that you can tailor the size of the tiles for the eventual decoration. We often decorate across many tiles, rather than decorating each one singly, so in the making stage we can cut tiles for specific areas, such as rectangular tiles for borders and even odd-shaped tiles for awkward corners. In fact, the more tile commissions we do, the more we opt to handmake our tiles because of this versatility.

Our tiles are made by the following method. We press the clay into a wooden frame slightly larger than the actual size of the finished tile, to allow for the clay shrinking. The frame has a false bottom. You can make the tile as deep as you like. We usually make our wall tiles about half an inch (1cm) thick, and 6 inches (15cm) square. We sometimes make very large tiles, but these can be prone to warping. Our floor tiles are a lot thicker, but we only produce a few handmade floor tiles as making acres and acres of them by hand can be very tedious in workshop conditions.

To make a tile frame, use strips of hardwood about half an inch (10mm) thick so that it will last. The bottom, which is loose, should be made from varnished marine ply about ⅛ inch (3mm) thick and should fit closely inside the frame. When making your frame, it is terribly important to remember that the

4 *Turn the terracotta tile out of the mould and on to a wooden drying pallet.*

5 *Put the pallet on a drying frame in a warm room. Turn the tiles after four days so that they dry evenly.*

depth of the frame must accommodate the depth of the tile required plus the false bottom. Cut as many false bottoms as you need as the tiles will be left to dry on them.

As with plate-making, make your tiles in batches because once you have prepared everything it is more efficient.

Once you have made your frame, make sure that you are working on a baseboard on a very firm and solid surface, and dust the baseboard with grog (powdered fired clay), sand or flint. Powdering the base in this way greatly facilitates the removal of the tile from the baseboard. Press the prepared clay into the mould, then cut away any excess with a cheese wire held taught against the sides of the frame. If there is not much excess, it can be scraped away with a metal ruler. Now smooth the surface with a rubber kidney. When the surface is smooth, push the baseboard, with the tile attached, up through the frame. Leave the tile to dry, watching out for warping. As with plates, the environment in which the tiles dry should not be too warm. Once they are bone dry – this usually takes a week – they can be biscuit fired, ready to glaze.

There is a great deal of scope for decorating a tile – decorating into and on to the wet or nearly dry clay, or with inlay sgraffito or slip decoration on to a white glaze, or using various forms of transfer decoration. We think that one of the best uses of handmade tiles is to make large panels and fire them with a white opaque glaze. The surface qualities are lovely.

6 *Remove edges from the tiles, tidy generally and smooth their top faces. Then they are ready to fire.*

A TILE PANEL OF DUCKS, CHICKENS, GEESE AND TURKEYS ON
HANDMADE 6-INCH (15CM) TILES.

BISCUIT FIRING

Until an object made from clay is fired, it cannot really be used. Several pieces of work can be fired together in a biscuit firing. There is a danger when glaze firing that the work will stick together, but when firing the biscuit you need only separate the pottery with pieces of fired clay.

There are two distinct firing phases in biscuit firing, the purpose of which is to bring the clay to its 'optimum' or recommended temperature. The first phase is the period where the water vapour chemically held within the clay is allowed to escape, this usually occurs between 100°C and 300°C (212 and 572°F). The second period burns away any organic or carbonaceous material. On average a biscuit firing in a medium-sized kiln should take about twelve hours, with the temperature rising on average no more than 100°C (212°F) per hour.

Once you have packed the kiln and closed the doors, but have left any vent holes or spy holes open to allow the steam to escape, turn the kiln on to its lowest setting. It should now be left until the temperature reaches between 200 and 350°C (392 and 662°F). This should take between three to six hours, depending on how many and how thick the plates or tiles are. When the kiln reaches this temperature you can fill the vent holes with bungs and turn the kiln to its medium setting.

After another three to four hours, the kiln should have reached a temperature of around 600°C (1112°F). You can now switch it to the highest setting where it can stay until the desired temperature is reached. Do take care that the increase in temperature is not too rapid.

When the firing is completed, turn the kiln off and allow to cool to well below 100°C (212°F) before you open the door or remove the bungs from the vents. Make sure that you do this very gradually as any sharp change in temperature will cause the fired clay to crack.

GLAZING

We will assume that the glaze is in a prepared form ready to be added to water. Most glazes are very poisonous before firing. It is advisable to wear a mask, available from your pottery supplier, when mixing glaze and it is important to keep hands clean and food and drink away from the glazing area. We keep overalls for glazing only and always remove them before leaving the studio.

If your glaze is in powder form you will need to mix it, either in a large plastic bucket, or in one of the tubs available from most pottery suppliers. Even if our glaze is pre-mixed, we always sieve it, first through a '120' and then an '80' sieve. If our glaze has been standing for some time we will re-sieve it through an 80, just to make absolutely sure there is nothing wrong with it. Any hairs or impurities would cause blemishes in the finish.

After adding water to the glaze, it should be the consistency of single cream. The thickness of the glaze is very important – you will learn by experience the consistency that's best – bearing in mind that the glaze must not be applied too thinly or too thickly.

We have found that the best method for glazing plates is to

1 Paint wax on the underside of the plate prior to glazing.

2 Pour the glaze through a sieve to make sure there are no impurities in it.

dip the biscuit pieces into the tub. It is relatively quick and deposits an even film over the surface. The time that the biscuit is immersed in the glaze depends on how liquid the glaze is and how porous the biscuit is. Tiles are skimmed over the surface of the glaze because only the face of the tile needs it.

In the firing of earthenware bodies, it is customary in small workshops to fire the clay just high enough to be hard, but not as high as its optimum firing temperature. This is because the more porous the pot or plate is at this stage, the easier it is to deposit a film of glaze on the piece. It is then followed by a commensurately higher temperature glaze firing so that the clay is finally fired to its correct temperature, at which point the glaze fuses to become a shiny, hard surface.

The problem with this procedure is that because the clay will not have reached its correct maturing temperature in the biscuit firing it is still relatively volatile, which might result in blemishes or pinholes as the gases try to find their way out from beneath the glaze. We have also found that this method often causes warping of large flat pieces.

We have solved this problem by firing our biscuit to a higher temperature than that of the glazed work to give us more control. The biscuit is less porous and in theory more difficult to glaze,

3 *Glaze one side of the tile by skimming it across the surface of the glaze.*
Allow the drips to run back into the bucket.

4 The plate is immersed in a tub of glaze for about seven seconds. Let the drips fall back into the glaze.

5 'Fettling' the plate – drips and finger marks are removed.

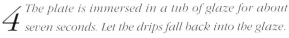

but there are substances called binders or flocculents that can be added to the glaze to increase glaze pick-up. Most suppliers will recommend what they call a glaze suspender which also solves the problem. Alternatively, calcium chloride may be added, and often bentonite as well, to stop the glaze from settling too quickly.

It is important to spend some time testing your bodies and glazes to establish what is going to work and what will not work. It is a pity to put a lot of time and effort into decorating a piece and have it fail in the firing process.

We paint a liquid wax emulsion to the bottom of our biscuits before we dip them to prevent the glaze adhering. Since our plates do not have a foot or a lip, this process is essential to stop the plate sticking to the kiln in firing. It may not be necessary if you are using a plate with a foot, because you can gently remove the glaze on the rim with a sponge or a piece of felt.

The conditions in your studio or workshop will determine how long it will be before the glazed plates are ready to decorate. In our case, it is about twelve hours. Before decoration, use a large brush to touch up areas where the plate was held while you were dipping it. Drip marks should be rubbed off gently with the fingers. Really difficult drips can be removed with a scouring pad.

Your plate or tile is now ready for decorating.

PLATES PLACED IN THE KILN READY FOR A
GLAZE FIRING.

GLAZE FIRING

Particular care must be taken in loading glazed ware into a kiln, as the glaze will fuse to everything it touches. Before you load your glazed ware into the kiln, it is important to paint your kiln shelves with batt wash, which is a mixture of powdered flint and fireclay and prevents any clays that might fall from sticking.

Tiles, where only the face is glazed, must be checked in case any glaze is lurking underneath. It is almost impossible to get a stuck tile out of the kiln in one piece. You can buy stilts or spurs for supporting glazed items. We fire our plates on stilts, even though there is no glaze on the bottom, as a precaution against sticking – it also allows air and heat to circulate during the firing.

Do make sure that you fire your kiln to the temperature recommended on the packet for the glaze. A glaze firing is not as critical as a

PLACING COMPLETED TILES IN CRANKS READY
FOR FIRING.

biscuit firing, where there is a lot of steam to control, but there is a definite procedure to be followed. After turning the kiln on we leave it at its lowest setting for three to four hours with all the bungs in and then we turn it to its medium setting for the same length of time. After that the kiln can be turned up to its highest setting until it reaches the required temperature. The average rise in temperature is about 100°C (212°F) an hour, but this can vary considerably, depending on how full the kiln is.

We 'soak' our glaze firing for half an hour after the required temperature is reached. 'Soaking' means keeping the kiln at the maximum temperature required for a period of time in order to allow the glaze to mature and settle. After this the kiln must be allowed to cool down to well below 100°C (212°F) before it is opened or any work removed – and remember to wear kiln gloves. If you empty your kiln too soon, your plates or tiles may well crack because of the shock caused by the sudden change of temperature.

TECHNIQUES
FOR APPLYING
PATTERN

❖

Inspiration, methods, materials, pattern and decoration are all inextricably linked. Design is a way of bringing all these elements together, a process of turning the inspiration into an idea and the idea into reality.

This book shows how our ideas and designs have developed and changed over the last ten years. It is always interesting to see how pattern starts to develop as you work hard at it and continue to experiment. We find that just by laying out colours and objects that inspire us something can be suggested that was not obvious when we started. Trying an idea out in cut paper, drawing and painting, cutting a lino block,

ALTHOUGH SPONGING HAS FOR A LONG TIME BEEN
USED RATHER LIKE POTATO PRINTING
OR RUBBER STAMPING, WE WERE FASCINATED
BY USING SPONGES TO PRODUCE MORE LIVELY
AND SPONTANEOUS TYPES OF DECORATION.
WE USE ONLY NATURAL SPONGES AND THIS
PICTURE SHOWS THE DEGREE OF
VERSATILITY AND VARIETY OF EFFECTS THAT
CAN BE ACHIEVED VERY SIMPLY.

76

A PHEASANT PLATTER IN BLUE WITH A
SGRAFFITO BOARDER.
A PHEASANT PLATE WITH A GREEN SPONGED
BORDER.

reducing and enlarging, all these things contribute to helping you to decide whether or not a particular pattern really works. More importantly, perhaps, it is enjoyable.

One day, by chance, a lady visiting our gallery told us that she had all her life painted traditional designs on to ceramics in Alsace, France. She much admired our work and we were interested to see what she would do on our plates. Before painting, she spent several minutes studying our unfamiliar plate, then, really concentrating, she swiftly executed a delightful design traditional to her region, with a circular rim exactly fitting the plate.

The delightful and spontaneous patterns that are produced in central Europe are very satisfying. What is their secret? Perhaps it is that there is a strong image on each plate. The design is repeated over and over again, but the spontaneity of execution gives the piece its special quality. I try to remember this when asked to paint a successful image yet again.

Whether we are designing for industry or for an individual customer, we welcome the constraints of the design brief, because it helps us to focus our mind on the matter. When we were asked to design and make a series of hunting, shooting and fishing platters for

STEEPLECHASE PATTERNS AND TILES SHOWN
WITH THE WORKING DRAWINGS.

A STEEPLECHASE PLATTER SURROUNDED BY
RIDING PARAPHERNALIA.

TULIP PLATE, BALLERINA TILE, BOAT AND
FISH TILE. A COLLECTION OF POTTERY
PAINTED BY A FIVE-YEAR-OLD CHILD.

the autumn promotion of a large London department store, we carefully considered our brief and came to the conclusion that we would develop a steeplechase in preference to hunting. We decided to develop game birds, such as pheasant and grouse, to represent shooting and then took a fresh look at our fish plates and developed a new range.

The illustration shows tiles and a plate painted by a five-year-old child. These interest us because strong design principles are already apparent. The tile, with its square border, shows a very traditional solution to the problem of designing for tiles, and the plate is joyous and colourful – the design is simple and satisfying and perfectly adapted to the form. Children's work is appealing, spontaneous and nearly always successful.

THE FRESHWATER PLATTER AND THE TEXTILES ARE COMMERCIALLY PRODUCED.

Autumn flowers displayed in a
sponged rose jug on our bakehouse
windowsill.

Opposite page: Pink, blue and yellow
add variety in this collection of
blue-and-white spongeware.

Below: Sponged plates.

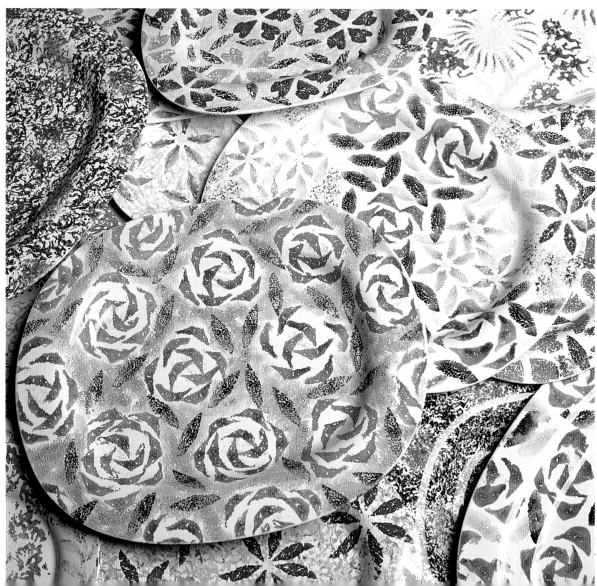

DECORATING THE UNFIRED CLAY

In order to put the techniques we use for our decoration into context it is useful to outline briefly some of the other methods of decorating pottery.

Whilst the clay is soft it can be stamped or impressed with objects raning from rope or leaves to patterned stamps cut from wood, plaster or fired clay. A fork or the point of a knitting needle can be used to scratch the design or it can be cut with a knife. Pieces of coloured clays or coiled clay can be pressed into the surface.

As the clay begins to dry, coloured liquid clay, called slip, can be painted, poured, or trailed over the surface to create patterns. Before drying, the slip can be combed, brushed or scratched through it, or used in conjunction with paper stencils to create decorative effects. The possibilites are endless and very different to those that we describe and use ourselves.

OVERGLAZE DECORATION OR 'MAJOLICA'

❖

All the hand decorating we do, and have illustrated in *Ceramic Style*, is achieved by working on to the unfired, raw glaze surface. The uniform white and durable surface is a wonderfully receptive surface on which to paint, and fulfils all our requirements. It is ideal for stencils, in particular, because it doesn't smudge easily.

An extremely important element in our work is that the designs, as well as the plates themselves, can be reproduced. Therefore, we have had to evolve methods of producing our ideas that make them easy to repeat, yet still mean that the designs are enjoyable and fun to decorate. For instance, we use stencils because they are an effective means of endlessly reproducing images and outlines, even though the real detailed work is being done by brushes, sponges and scratching into the glazed surface. The result is that, although we could faithfully reproduce ideas exactly, we prefer to make them slightly different. This is probably best illustrated in our series of cockerels or fish, where the image remains constant but the composition and emphasis change dramatically from one plate to another.

ROSES AND ROSE PLATTER

DRAWING

❖

Most of our ideas are evolved from drawing or working on paper first; at this stage all the criteria involved in translating the idea on to a plate or tile are thought about. Having decided on the imagery which in this instance, for example, will be a fish, we then consider whether it should work as a border or cover most of the plate, and whether there should be

A COLLECTION OF DRAWINGS, TILES AND LINOCUTS RELATING TO OUR FARM THEME.

HOLLYLEAF PLATES SHOWN WITH THEIR
DRAWINGS.

one fish or different fish or indeed other
imagery. We rather like flatfish because there is
plenty of scope for decorating in and around its
shape. Having decided on a particular type of
fish, we then spend time drawing it. Through
the drawing we begin to understand what
features make that particular fish special – for
example, what distinguishes the grey mullet
from the sea bream.

One of the most useful tools in our studio is
our photocopier, because it enables us to
enlarge and reduce our drawings which saves
hours of tedious work. This effectively means we
can tailor imagery to different sizes.

Sometimes it takes many drawings to achieve
a result one is happy with. At this stage, sheets
of layout paper (paper that you can see through)
are useful because they can be overlaid on to the
basic drawing, and the line and form perfected
without having to start from the beginning over
and over again.

A JUMBLE OF SEASHORE OBJECTS SHOWING THE
STENCILS CUT FOR FISH.

MAKING A STENCIL

❖

For something like a flatfish we use three stencils. One outlines the shape and probably includes any distinguishing lines likes eyes or gills, another outlines the fins and tail, and the last is a negative stencil that allows the inside of the fish shape to be coloured.

In order that the stencil paper can be cut accurately, put a piece of carbon paper between the two and follow the final fish drawing. Any other imagery to be included, like seaweed or shells, can be treated in the same way.

Having decided on the size of the image and the plate, it is now a question of how best to apply the colour and by what means to achieve the desired surface qualities. Our flatfish platter described on pages 118-121 gives some ideas.

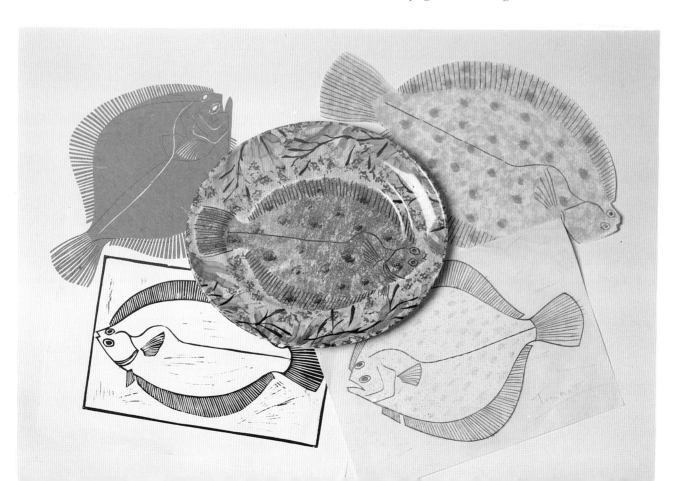

PARTRIDGE PLATE.

OPPOSITE: A FLATFISH PLATTER WITH ALL ITS
STENCILS AND A LINOCUT.

SPONGING

❖

We use only natural sponges – both the fine ones and the larger, coarser types. Fine sponges produce a delicate stipple-like quality which is marvellous, for instance, for building up colour in a fish or bird. Sponges have a wonderful ability to hold just the right amount of colour so that, with practice, you can impart it on to the surface evenly.

It is not surprising that cut-and-tied sponged decoration provided an industry all its own for a period in the nineteenth century. Fine old examples exist, and it is still being produced. It is synonymous with a certain kind of rural pottery – it would have been cheap to produce because of the restriction in the scale of pattern. As a technique on its own it could be considered rather dull and limiting. Nevertheless sponging has an unmistakable character – and whether the whole sponge is used to decorate a plate or part of the sponge is used in the background, they are a very useful tool.

1 A fine petal-shaped sponge is gently dabbed to produce five petals for each rose. As the plate has both pink and lilac coloured roses, areas must be left for each. The same petal-shaped sponge is used to produce both the lilac and pink roses.

2 The centre of each rose is decorated with a coarse natural sponge in yellow.

3 A fine sponge is used to stipple in a turquoise background. The leaf sponge is dabbed on to the background between the roses to complete the plate.

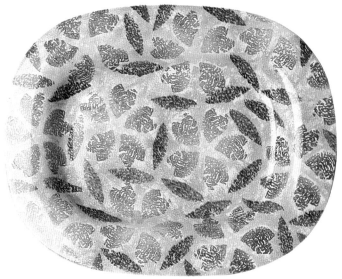

Michaelmas Daisy platter

Materials required: coarse natural sponge for rose centres, cut fine sponge in form of flower petal, cut sponge in form of simple leaf, fine sponge for background. Pink, lilac, turquoise, yellow and green glaze stains.

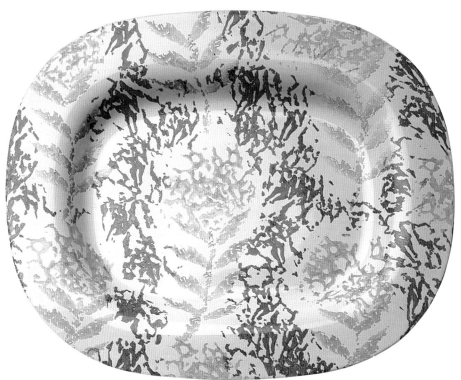

Another sponged flower design developed for fast production. Blue has been dabbed on with a sponge.

A COLOURFUL DISPLAY OF OUR FLORAL SPONGEWARE DESIGNS
DEVELOPED TO BE QUICK TO DECORATE WHILST BEING BOLD
AND LIVELY.

SGRAFFITO

❖

We very rarely use this technique to scratch through the opaque glaze, but we often scratch through a colour that has been painted on top revealing the white underneath. On many of our early blue-and-white plates we would scratch through the predominantly blue background for white centres or stems of plants. More recently we have used the technique in our black-and-white zoo plates, where we scratch into the black areas we have painted but following the inside lines of the stencil. This has the effect of softening the image and creating an almost etched quality. In the same series the borders are also scratched to produce a rather primitive finish to the work.

ANTELOPE PLATE WITH SCRATCHED BORDER. A SCRATCHED LINE HAS BEEN DRAWN AROUND THE INSIDE OF THE STENCIL TO GIVE THE IMAGE AN ETCHED QUALITY.

THE BORDER AND THE BODY OF THE ZEBRA HAVE BEEN SCRATCHED THROUGH, REVEALING THE WHITE UNDERNEATH.

93

BRUSHES

A lot of time can go into selecting brushes. Different brushes are made to perform very different tasks, – their construction more or less suggests what can or cannot be done with them. Certainly we have found that looking through them is the best way of finding what we want because pottery suppliers list their brushes under all kinds of different names. Do buy the best quality that you can afford, and make sure that the brush you buy is the best for its purpose. It is the hairs that do the work, and as with all materials, different hairs behave in different ways.

In our studio we use brushes for two functions – for drawing lines, or for applying small or large areas of colour. For the latter we use both flat and round brushes, sable and a great variety of other hairs, and all sizes. Experimenting will soon reveal which achieves the best result. Drawing brushes are more complex. All ours come from Italy, where the technique of majolica is still carried out in a small commercial way, as they are very difficult to obtain anywhere else. We have listed one supplier in the United Kingdom (see page 156), but failing all else you could make your own by shaping an ordinary brush with fine scissors. They are best described as an ordinary sable brush with what appear to be the hairs of a much finer brush protruding from the end. The fine hairs draw a line fed from the larger head which acts as a reservoir for the colour. These brushes come in a variety of sizes, depending on the thickness of line one wishes to draw, and their advantage is that you can draw a continuous line without the colour blobbing.

DECORATING A HYPERICUM BLUE-AND-WHITE PLATE. THIS ILLUSTRATES
THE USE OF A LARGE SOFT MOP-TYPE BRUSH FOR PAINTING
BACKGROUND AND A FINER BRUSH FOR PAINTING LINES IN THE PETALS.

TILE PANEL OF THE VIEW OF THE GARDEN AT
CRANBORNE MANOR.

FREEHAND PAINTING

Before you paint directly on to the surface, it is useful to familiarize yourself with the image that you are going to paint.

We search for images that we consider have a universal appeal – one that is familiar to most people, friendly and seen time and time again: an avenue of trees, jugs of flowers, fruit, animals. These images are all endlessly interesting to us.

We do not tire of 'worrying' these ideas. For example, Wendy has painted the avenue of arched apple trees many times on ceramic tile panels as well as weaving the view on tapestry – dyeing each coloured yarn before use – and has learnt from each attempt. Once an image is learnt, it is easier to execute it quickly, which is advantageous when decorating ceramics.

Painting majolica is quite a challenge. The colours are not as brilliant as they will appear when fired – cobalt blue appears to be black, for instance, and the blotting-paper surface of the unfired glaze absorbs the stain. Try to keep the final result that you are hoping to achieve in your mind at all times. It is also worth trying really hard to avoid damage to the glaze surface or having over-thick paint that will bubble in firing. Majolica has an advantage over underglaze methods of decoration because if the idea has failed, you can wash the glaze off and start again.

When freehand painting, you need to give some thought as to how the plate will look before you start. The country hedgerows and orchards that abound in our area provide wonderful forms to paint. The colours of autumn are also very pleasing after the brighter shapes of summer. We call a whole range of plates that we do 'Apple Plates', but in reality they depict medlars, quinces, blackberries and any variety of autumn fruits and berries.

We heap the fruit and branches on the table and then paint directly on to the plate or tiles – the design varies from plate to plate. After a time we find some compositions are more pleasing than others. At this point it is time to formalize the design. We sometimes use the pinpricking method of transferring the design that we saw being used in Deruta, Italy The correct term for this is 'pouncing'.

WOVEN TAPESTRY BY WENDY OF THE POTAGER AT CRANBORNE MANOR, DORSET, IN EARLY SUMMER WITH THE APPLE BLOSSOM IN FULL FLOWER.

A TYPICAL AUTUMN SIGHT IN OUR PART OF NORMANDY. THE CIDER APPLES HAVE BEEN COLLECTED WHERE THEY HAVE FALLEN AND PILED INTO HEAPS IN THE FIELDS READY TO BE PRESSED.

1 *Cider apples and eating apples being painted by Wendy. A palette of colours – ochres, rusts and greens – has been selected and the centre of the plate is being worked on.*

2 *Many of Wendy's plates are composed without any preliminary paintings or drawings. Sometimes there is no substitute for a more spontaneous approach. Many of her series of plates evolve in this way.*

3 *Working on the border with the centre of the plate almost complete.*

4 *Wendy scratching into her painting, almost drawing into the painted areas to emphasize and clarify certain elements.*

THREE 10-INCH (25CM) APPLE PLATES IN THE APPLE STORE.

99

POUNCING OR PINPRICKING

Using the pinprick method to transfer your design on to the glazed ceramic piece gives an outline that can be used either as a guide or to follow faithfully. It is especially useful if a set of plates is required that are 'similar but different', or indeed for repetition in the case of breakage or a glaze fault.

We decided to pounce this sketch. The method is very simple. Place the tracing paper over the sketch, which you have fixed with masking tape to a soft surface that you can pinprick into. We use a felt pad, but soft cardboard or polystyrene could be used. We also use brooch pins rather than dressmakers' pins as they give the right size of hole needed to press the powdered charcoal through.

In this instance, we had painted the original view to the size of the plates, once for a large platter and again for the small one. With any sketch that you wish to transfer, it is a good idea to redraw it or paint it to size. This way you not only save your original – it also makes it a good deal simpler to transfer.

How you choose to interpret your drawing is up to you. Our method is to pinprick the line that we wish to paint in cobalt as an outline. Then we paint in the other colours and tones using the original sketch as a guide. This method of outlining in blue, maganese or black was used in Dutch majolica patterns and is called trek.

Once you have pricked all the lines you require as a guide, lift the tracing paper from the original. To check that you have all the information you will need, place it over a sheet of paper and take an impression. To do this, first grind some charcoal with a pestle and mortar into a fine powder and then make a little bag of powdered charcoal. We use fine Terylene or muslin tied tightly with string. Then dab the bag on to the tracing paper keeping close to the lines. This is messy, so it is sensible to wear an overall. It is a good idea to keep sketches and pinpricked tracings apart once the tracing has been used, as the charcoal

spreads. The pinpricked tracing can be used over and over again until it wears out.

If you have what you want in the first impression you can proceed to the glazed plate or tiles, where the method is exactly the same. It can be quite tricky to hold the tracing paper down on a plate with a rim. Use masking tape if you can. Once you have taken the impression, paint the outline.

Decorating plates is good fun, particularly with the methods and techniques we describe, but it is important to experiment in order to learn for yourself what is and what is not possible. We never decorate anything without a few glazed tiles on hand on which to try out a brush or sponge, making sure the colour flows satisfactorily, or the sponge is not too wet or dry. However, the great advantage of on-glaze decoration is that if it goes wrong you can wash it off, and start all over again.

THE ESSENTIAL ELEMENTS OF THE ORIGINAL DRAWINGS HAVE NOW BEEN PAINTED ON TO THE PLATE FOLLOWING THE LINES OF CHARCOAL THAT HAVE BEEN POUNCED OR DABBED THROUGH THE PINPRICKED AREAS. THE MATERIALS, DRAWINGS AND BRUSHES ARE SHOWN AROUND THE PLATE.

MATERIALS REQUIRED: TISSUE PAPER, SHARP NEEDLE, THIMBLE, CHARCOAL, WATER-COLOUR PAINT OR GOUACHE, PESTLE AND MORTAR, MUSLIN, LAYOUT PAD, PENCILS.

1 Place the pinpricked tracing paper, with the design in position, over the glazed tiles.

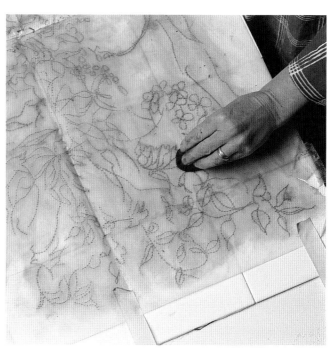

2 Pounce the pinpricked area of the composition with fine charcoal wrapped in muslin.

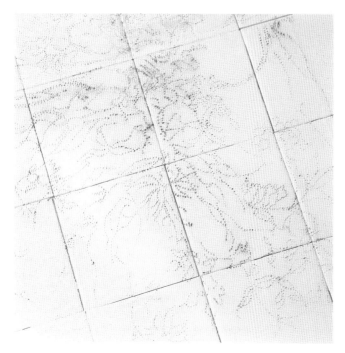

3 The tissue paper has been removed carefully, leaving the charcoal impression of the composition.

4 Wendy is now painting into the composition using the charcoal impression as a guide.

A WORKING DRAWING
THAT HAS BEEN TRACED
FROM WENDY'S ORIGINAL.
ALL THE IMPORTANT
ELEMENTS HAVE BEEN
PINPRICKED.

THE COMPLETED PLATE.

103

THEMES &
PROJECTS

❖

The subjects we discuss and illustrate in this chapter show the way in which we work and how some of our designs have evolved. These subjects are, for us, extremely inspirational – each evokes reactions, different colours and imagery.

Research and observation are both very important. It is interesting how often you think you may know what a particular object looks like because you visualize it so clearly in your mind; when you come to put it down on paper, you discover all the difficulties. There is no substitute for sitting down and really looking at the subject while you draw it. This is particularly true of plants and flowers where the subtle differences in colour and shape are vitally important. Cottage garden flowers and wild meadow flowers are subjects full of evocative imagery, but how to reproduce them in practical terms is not always an easy question. What is it that makes them evocative? What are the colours, and what are the basic shapes?

This collection of paintings and drawings of flowers illustrates Wendy's spontaneous approach to the subject.

104

THE COCKEREL IS A VERY STRONG IMAGE. IN
THIS PICTURE TILES, DRAWINGS, FABRICS AND
LINOCUTS ARE BROUGHT TOGETHER IN A RICH
JUMBLE TO EMPHASIZE THE ENJOYMENT THAT
CAN BE DERIVED FROM EXPERIMENTING ACROSS
A WIDE RANGE OF MEDIUMS.

In contrast to a figurative painter or photographer who replicate what they see, a designer has to analyse and scrutinize the subject, take it apart element by element, and re-create the essence of it. It helps to look at the subject in lots of different ways. Although we do a lot of preliminary drawings, we also use photographs, cut paper, stencils – anything that holds another dimension. By putting all this visual information together, all kinds of other different ideas and patterns are suggested that would otherwise not have come to mind. You cannot expect things to start to happen, or begin to work, if you do not put the work in initially.

As you spend time on your image and ideas begin to develop in new directions your reference material becomes ever richer as new elements appear. Although *Ceramic Style* is about decoration on pottery, much of the enjoyment we derive from experimenting and trying out our ideas comes from making all kinds of other objects as well. Each craft has its own possibilities and characteristics, but the process by which ideas are realized remains the same. What we are trying to achieve in our work, whether in ceramics, textiles or anything else, is a rich juxtaposition of colour, shape and pattern, using not only different themes and designs jumbled up together, but also different techniques and methods.

What is achievable or not on ceramics is only part of the picture. We could not envisage restricting our ideas to just one dimension – it is the variety and richness that interest us. The same themes and influences that inspire our ceramic work, inspire our work in other media too.

The step-by-step projects on the following pages show how we have used favourite themes to develop our ceramic style.

A PAINTED STUDY OF FRESH FLOWERS.

ONE OF A SERIES OF DUCK PLATES WITH
SPONGED AND PAINTED DECORATION
PHOTOGRAPHED FLOATING ON A WEED-
COVERED POND.

THE
FARMYARD

❖

As modern living becomes ever more sophisticated and predictable, the romanticism attached
to the countryside and the suggestion of a life of
serenity and stability can have tremendous appeal.

Unfortunately mechanization has deprived us
of some of farming's most evocative imagery –
many activities no longer involve either human
labour or horses. Somehow a tractor or a combine
harvester does not quite evoke the same
atmosphere as a team of shire horses or a group
of reapers. Nor does a field of large cylindrical
bales of straw have the same effect as a field of
stooked corn; but a ploughed field looks much
the same whatever method is used.

There are lots of images associated with the
farm. Individual images such as cows, sheep,
chickens, goats and pigs can look great if you
bring them together: we use a mixture of these
farmyard elements to create a country look on
our ceramics. Just as inspirational is the farming
calendar, which follows the seasons: spring
planting, summer growing, autumn harvesting,
winter ploughing, each suggesting its own
special palette. Traditionally the harvest, because
it is the culmination of the farmer's year, is
associated with some of the strongest colours
and images. Some designers have created
wonderful harvest mugs and plates using rust,
browns, golden yellows and oranges, the colours
of dry corn, baked bread and autumn.

We have chosen to give step-by-step instruc-
tions on how we decorate a cockerel plate,
because the cockerel is such a well-loved image.

DEVON FARM, A LARGER AND MORE COLOURFUL RANGE THAN
CAROUSEL, COMPRISING MANY DIFFERENT FARM ANIMALS.

CAROUSEL, ONE OF OUR FARMYARD DESIGNS, DEVELOPED IN OUR
STUDIOS BY HAND-DECORATING METHODS, BUT NOW PRODUCED IN A
FACTORY.

110

AN EARLY SPONGED TILE PANEL OF CHICKENS, DUCKS AND GEESE.

A PAINTED COCKEREL WITH SPONGED
BACKGROUND AND SPONGED AND BANDED
BORDER.

NO OTHER CREATURE IS MORE
SYNONYMOUS WITH THE FARMYARD THAN
THE COCKEREL.

1 The stencil is placed on the tile and a pale grey, light wash of colour is painted on to the body using a medium-sized sable brush.

2 The grey area is then sponged very delicately with black stain using a fine sponge to imitate fine features.

3 The legs and feet area of the stencil are also painted through with black.

4 Paint through the tail portion of the stencil with black paint.

5 The bill and comb are painted red using a soft fine brush through a stencil cut for this purpose.

6 A slightly coarser fragment of fine sponge is used to dab green around the feet for the grass, and the beak of the cock is carefully painted black using an extremely fine majolica brush.

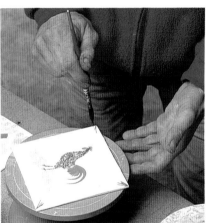

7 Lines are painted on all four corners using a fine brush.

1 *The cockerel is painted through a stencil in two parts – the body, and the comb and bill. It is important when placing the stencil to allow for the comb. The first colour is painted through the body using a soft flat brush.*

2 *The next colour is painted through the tail section of the stencil and the feet, legs and wing lines are painted using a fine brush.*

3 *The second part of the stencil is used to paint through the red bill and comb, and a fine majolica brush is used to paint the beak.*

4 *A fine sponge is used to dab on the green areas for the grass. A large soft mop-type brush is used to band the yellow area and a finer majolica brush to produce the fine dark bands.*

MATERIALS REQUIRED:
FINE SPONGES AND BRUSHES,
COBALT OXIDES AND GLAZE STAIN,
TWO-PART STENCIL.

A FINE SELECTION OF COCKEREL
PLATES SHOWING THE DIVERSITY
OF DECORATION, ARRANGED ON
ONE OF OUR OWN PLATE RACKS IN
OUR BARN.

THIS PAINTING BY HARRIET BARBER TYPIFIES
THE NORMANDY SEASCAPE CLOSE TO WHERE
WE LIVE.

THE SEA

We have both always lived fairly near the sea, but since we moved to northern France it seems to have had an even greater influence on our work. We are more aware of it because it is so near to our house and forms an important part of our local landscape. The sea appears to play a very prominent role in the lives of our local community, many of whom are involved in one way or another with what is harvested from it. You are as likely to see an ancient tractor pulling a trailer full of oysters as carrots or cauliflowers.

Whether or not one is fortunate enough to have it close by, the idea of the sea nevertheless stimulates and evokes all kinds of visual and sensory reactions in many people. It certainly brings to mind a particular palette of colours. Seaweeds are numerous and incredibly varied in form and often beautifully coloured, especially as they lie on the sand, wet between tides. Their colours can range from coral and purplish pinks through reddish browns, ochres and rusts to an even larger range of greens. Seaweed has a strong imagery, and is fun to draw and paint. We find it particularly useful as a border decoration for tiles or plates. As our working photographs show, wonderful watery almost translucent qualities can be achieved when oxides are brushed through seaweed stencils.

Sea themes are particularly relevant as decorative features in the bathroom and kitchen. Seafood looks especially good when it is served on decorative fish plates. Practical considerations like the length and shape of fish dictate the shape of the plate, but if it complements the food, its presentation is much enhanced.

A FLATFISH FITS NEATLY ON THE BOTTOM OF THE PLATE AND
SPONGING IS USED SUCCESSFULLY WITH CRABS AND SHRIMPS TO
ENLIVEN IT.

117

1 The open stencil of the fish is placed carefully on to the plate and fine sponges are used to gently stipple three or four separate colours forming the body of the fish. Each colour is applied in turn over the whole surface, the lightest colour first.

2 The open stencil is replaced with the solid line stencil, and a fine majolica brush used to paint black lines through the cut areas for fins, gills, tail, and so on.

3 With all the lines painted, the line stencil can be removed and any lines needing attention painted very carefully freehand.

4 The line stencil is replaced with the solid stencil to cover and protect all previously decorated areas. The background is now stippled with any variety of sea colours, using the fine sponges.

5 The solid stencil is carefully removed and a fine sponge selected to put dots of colour into the fish – dabs of rust or ochre are associated with fish such as plaice.

119

6 The border of this particular plate has a rather random collection of seaweed painted over the fine sponged areas. We generally paint through the largest of the stencils first with a wide soft brush to give rather a watery wash of colour.

7 Finer stencils are used on top to create a tangled quality.

8 As a final touch, coarse sponges are used gently to apply colour in a way that suggests ripples.

THE DECORATED PLATE.

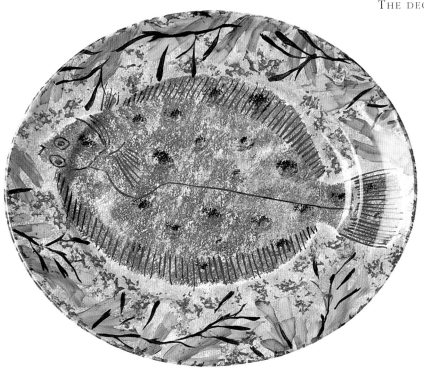

121

1 *Tiles are particularly good for trying out ideas – in this series of photographs the seaweed stencils are being used as a guide only. The colour is applied more as a wash than as solid colour, and the more tones of the same colour or mixes of colours, such as greens, the better.*

2 *The largest of the stencils is used to paint through the various shades of green.*

3 *A smaller stencil has been placed over the first stencil and is painted through in parts.*

4 *The finer stencil is now overlaid and again only painted in parts to suggest a tangled, moving mass of seaweed.*

THE FINISHED SEAWEED TILE.

EXPERIMENTAL TILES AND SMALL PLATES ARE USEFUL FOR TRYING OUT
IDEAS AND COLOURS.

123

FLOWERS

❖

WORKING ON A PROJECT INVOLVES MANY HOURS OF EXPERIMENTING AND TRYING OUT IDEAS. SWEET PEAS ARE THE CENTRAL THEME HERE – THIS PICTURE SHOWS THE DRAWINGS, STENCILS AND COLOURS INVOLVED IN ARRIVING AT A SATISFACTORY CONCLUSION.

The use of flowers as imagery for decoration of ceramics, textiles and woodcarvings has a long and varied history. A book of reproductions of artist's flower paintings shows a great variety of styles and is a source of inspiration. Indian crewel work, chintz and William Morris fabrics all take flowers as their starting point, but are widely different in style and technique. We try to

have jugs of fresh flowers in the house at all times, either grown specially or gathered from the wild area of the garden.

There is only a very short period of the year when we need to use dried flowers to provide the colours that we love. We are lucky enough to have a field that we have planted with cornflowers, marigolds, clarkia and poppies. It looks spectacular in June and provides masses of flowers for picking and drying.

Our idea for our first floral designs for ceramic production was to build up a series of flowers used singly on separate plates that would give a bunched effect when mixed together on the dresser or the table. We preferred this at the time to mixing them all together on one piece. We are now developing designs which

A LATE SUMMER SETTING OF TULIP ARRANGED FOR TEA BENEATH A COPPER BEECH WITH A CARPET OF WILD PINK CYCLAMEN IN A FRENCH GARDEN.

125

DESIGNING WITH CUT COLOURED PAPERS RATHER THAN PAINTING OR
DRAWING CAN BE AN EXTREMELY INTERESTING WAY OF DEVELOPING
IDEAS.

use seasonal flowers together such as spring bulbs or meadow flowers. For us, the development of ideas involves drawing the flowers accurately as they become available and painting studies of mixtures and colour combinations.

If you are working on a floral design, try to get hold of the flowers themselves, as this will help you to capture their character. If this is not possible, use books of botanical prints, postcard reproductions or anything you can lay your hands on to help you to develop your ideas.

Flowers lend themselves to a very freehand, painterly approach, but also to a more disciplined approach. The tulip, one of our favourites, is treated quite formally on the tessera plate shown here, but really runs wild on a tile panel we painted for a farmhouse kitchen.

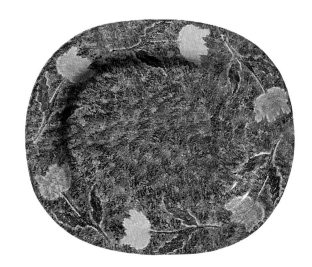

TESSERA TULIP PLATTER.

MANY OF OUR TILE PANELS ARE SUCCESSFULLY USED BEHIND COOKERS, LIKE THIS WONDERFUL DISPLAY OF HAND-PAINTED WILD FLOWERS.

1 In our tessera tulip three colours are used in the background – turquoise, blue and black – through three stencils.

2 Each colour is applied with a fine natural sponge producing an all-over fine stipple background.

3 A medium-blue cobalt is sponged over the turquoise.

4 Finally the black is applied, sparingly, more to give interest than colour. The positive stencils are then removed, revealing the white beneath.

5 *The open tulip stencils are now carefully placed over the space left by the solid stencils.*

6 *Green is applied with a fine sponge into the leaf and stem area of the stencil.*

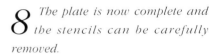

7 *Each petal area of the tulip is now sponged with a different colour.*

8 *The plate is now complete and the stencils can be carefully removed.*

MATERIALS REQUIRED:
TULIP (STENCILS POSITIVE AND
NEGATIVE), FINE SPONGES, TURQUOISE
STAIN, BLACK STAIN, COBALT OXIDE,
YELLOW STAIN, PINK STAIN, BRUSHES
AND BOWLS FOR MIXING COLOUR, AND
GLAZED TILES FOR TESTING
CONSISTENCY AND SHADE OF COLOUR
AND TEXTURE OF SPONGE.

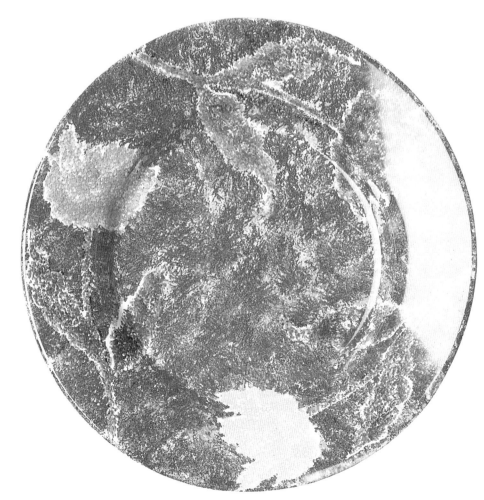

TULIP PLATE.

OUR TULIP AND STEEPLECHASE DESIGNS WORK VERY WELL TOGETHER
ON A DRESSER IN OUR SHOWROOM.

1 *Five stencils are placed evenly half on the rim and half in the centre of the plate. The lighter of the two blues is brushed over each stencil in turn towards the middle of the plate.*

2 *Holding the stencil carefully in the same position, the back of a natural sponge is used to stipple over the stencils on the rim of the plate in the darker of the two blues.*

3 *With the border complete, the positive stencils are removed and the open part of the stencil is used to paint through the lighter of the two blues on to the part of the vine leaf resting on the rim.*

4 *To finish, a line is scratched on the centre of the vine leaf between the white and the blue to emphasize the centre. As a final flourish a loop suggesting a vine is scratched between each vine leaf on the stippled border.*

THIS SMALL VINE-LEAF PLATTER HAS BEEN SPONGED, STENCILLED, PAINTED AND SCRATCHED IN TWO SHADES OF COBALT BLUE.

MATERIALS REQUIRED: FIVE VINE-LEAF STENCILS (POSITIVE AND NEGATIVE), SOFT-MOP TYPE BRUSH PALE AND DARK MIX OF COBALT OXIDE, NATURAL SPONGE TO PRODUCE STIPPLE (USE THE BACK SIDE) AND A SHARP INSTRUMENT (KNITTING NEEDLE OR TAPESTRY BOBBIN, FOR EXAMPLE) FOR SCRATCHING.

VINE LEAF AND SPONGEWARE IN A FARMHOUSE APPLE STORE, GLOUCESTERSHIRE.

ZOO ANIMALS & EXOTIC BIRDS

A zoo houses many types of creatures – colourful birds, butterflies, snakes and insects; also highly patterned animals such as zebras and leopards and some that are spectacular for the grace of their movement. We also think of rainforests, jungles, the tropics, semi-desert bushland, African savannah and plains. There is another ingredient, too – the human element. Evocative terms like tribal, primitive, ethnic or nomadic come to mind. The words bushland and savannah evoke browns, rusts and ochres, and tropical birds and jungles suggest emerald greens, pinks and purples.

As with flowers, butterflies and insects, the varieties and combinations of colours associated with birds are very exciting, and the names are as extraordinary and extravagant as the birds themselves – the African paradise flycatcher, the yellow-breasted boatbill or the long-tailed manakin.

There are very few historical ceramic references for exotic birds other than on some highly ornate German and French porcelain and, occasionally, as a very minor decorative detail, on Chinese-inspired blue-and-white willow patterns. Strangely enough, exotic birds seem to be an extremely rare occurrence, given the strong tradition that exists of bird illustration. One cannot help wondering why Thomas Bewick's engravings of English birds, or the work of John Gould or John James Audubon, were never reproduced in any form on plates.

Bird plates are something of a challenge as

A COLLECTION OF OUR ZOO PLATES WITH SPONGED, SCRATCHED AND
BANDED BORDERS.

135

A COLOURFUL DISPLAY OF YELLOW-BORDERED BIRD PLATES WITH BLUE-AND-WHITE FLOWER PLATES.

the imagery is incredibly strong and colourful, but it can be difficult to make it work. The elements that characterize one type of bird from another, apart from size and colouring – the definite places, trees and plants we associate certain birds with – dictate how best that particular bird should be portrayed. There are birds we associate with, for example, the sea, the English countryside, forests, mountains and Australian rivers. Without doubt a jungle suggests a toucan or macaw, in the same way

136

that the farmyard suggests turkeys and geese, and a cage, sadly, a canary or myna bird.

Some birds have a particular significance attached to them through folklore and custom. The cockerel is a good example; it is not only a strong symbol and part of French culture and society but also typifies rural life and the farmyard. We once had a request from a Canadian customer for 'loon' bird plates. At the time we had no idea that the loon was as important in Canadian tradition as the maple leaf, or any idea that it was a black-throated diver. It is important to be able to construct a design not just from the obvious and from what is in front of you, but also by researching and looking beyond, finding many other possible ingredients.

Our interpretation of the zoo evokes strong ethnic, primitive and tribal feelings, through the associations and the colour. When we think of a zoo, we think of very specific animals: elephants, rhinos, giraffes and zebras, and colours such as sand colours, terracottas, browns, rusts, greys and blacks. These colours evoke primitive forms of animal interpretation – for instance the extraordinary French cave paintings at Lascaux with their images of bison, horses and reindeer in rusts and charcoal greys, and the scratched line drawings and the strange qualities of sienna pigment rubbed into the surface of the cave itself. Here the means by which the drawings or paintings have been executed is an integral part of the strength of the images. We have also collected a wonderful example of an African resist-dyed indigo fabric; the imagery includes snakes, lizards, tigers, birds and fishes. What is striking about this fabric, like many African fabrics, are its wonderful lines, an almost etched feeling. In our black-and-white zoo series, which

137

A SELECTION OF WORKING DRAWINGS,
COLOURS AND IDEAS. THE TOUCAN IN THE
LEFT-HAND CORNER WAS CONSTRUCTED FROM
COLOURED PAPER, AND FURTHER IDEAS
DEVELOPED AS WE CONTINUED TO EXPERIMENT.

A COLLECTION OF DUCK PLATES BESIDE WATER.

A SELECTION OF BLACK-AND-WHITE ANIMAL
PLATES WITH BOTH SCRATCHED AND BANDED
BORDERS.

we are still developing, we wanted to achieve a similar effect. The images are produced by painting solid colour through a stencil and then very carefully, with the stencil still in place, scratching a line – with an old compass or knitting needle – following the inside contour of the stencil. The border is treated in a similar manner and is also scratched.

African textiles and imagery contain a wealth of influences, as do Indian textiles where animals and birds feature even more prominently. Whether it is textiles or cave paintings, Cretan pottery or North American Indian baskets, these elements have influenced our designs and ideas and are an extremely important part of our work.

141

A COLLECTION OF OBJECTS ILLUSTRATING HOW
OUR IDEAS DEVELOP AND CHANGE OVER A
PERIOD OF TIME. STENCILS, WAX, CRAYONS,
LINO BLOCKS AND FABRICS ARE ONLY PART OF
THE PROCESS OF EXPLORING A THEME.

DETAIL OF A HAND-PAINTED TILE PANEL
OF WILD FLOWERS BEHIND AN AGA IN A
COUNTRY KITCHEN.

DECORATIVE TILES

❖

The hygienic, waterproof surface makes tiles the obvious choice for kitchens and bathrooms. One often encounters a nervousness about the use of colour and decoration on tiles in these rooms, but where this is overcome we have seen some stunning results, among these a simple patchwork of tiles painted by children and placed behind an Aga.

In Turkey a riot of decorative tiles is used on buildings. Looking at these instilled in us a love of tile decoration. Patterns border other patterns, and each addition enhances the last.

There is a strong tradition of tiles and decorative tile pictures in Europe, centred mainly in Spain and Portugal. Around the beginning of the sixteenth century, migrant Italian majolica painters visited Spain and set up tile-painting workshops. The fashion spread to Holland by the end of the century. Soon these brightly coloured tile pictures were superseded by a predominantly blue-and-white palette, producing increasingly sophisticated results. This change was probably influenced by the fashion for blue-and-white porcelain imported from China.

The subject matter for Dutch tile panels was flowers, decorative landscapes, seascapes, hunting scenes, town views, allegories and chinoiserie. In Holland small tile panels were frequently used for decorative and descriptive house signs.

Such was the skill of the European tile painters that they were able to produce completely

realistic effects, called trompe l'oeil literally 'fooling the eye'. We came across a particularly striking example in the National Museum of Decorative Arts in Madrid – a whole room of tiles painted in naive style depicting a pantry. In this painted room, cooks, maids and footmen scurry about carrying trays of delicious food. Decorative birds hang from the walls and the shelves are laden with delicious fare. We often

OLD AND NEW FRENCH STENCILLED TILES AND KITCHEN RANGE FORM AN INTERESTING BACKDROP FOR OUR STUDIO PLATES.

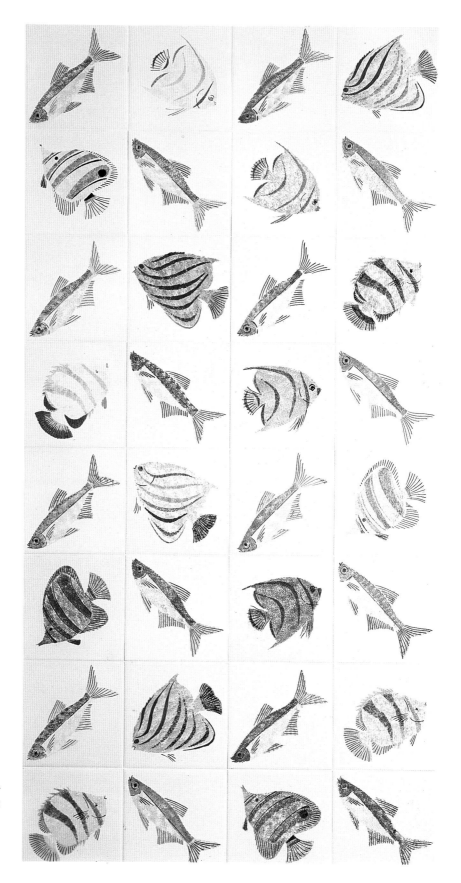

THE PANEL COMMISSIONED BY
BOURNEMOUTH MUSEUM TO
COMMEMORATE THE OPENING OF A
NEW GALLERY. A DECORATIVE FISH
DESIGN SEEMED APPROPRIATE AS
THE MUSEUM OVERLOOKS THE
SEA.

146

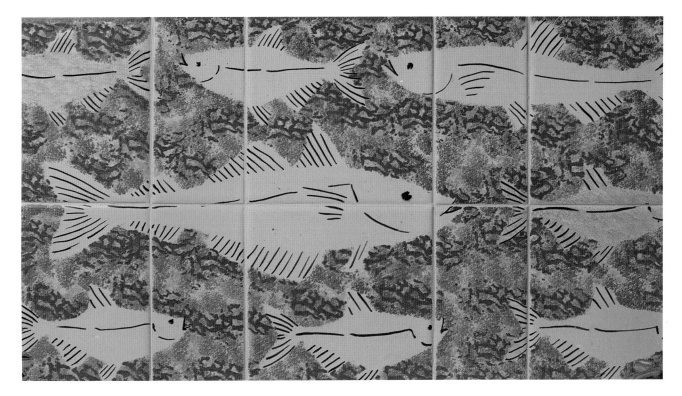

use this trompe l'oeil technique and once added a 'window', complete with curtains, vase of flowers and baskets of fruit, to bring life to a particularly dingy room.

Decorative tile panels and pictures are very often successfully used as back-drops for cookers and stoves. Interestingly, there is also a tradition in northern Europe of using tiles to cover the stove itself. These are often splendidly decorated.

We are very fond of the blue-and-white tiled kitchens that are found fairly frequently in France – a well-known example that is open to the public is the kitchen in Claude Monet's house at Giverny.

We enjoy working within this decorative tradition, but we interpret the style in our own way and do not copy the originals exactly. If you need to cover a large area with tiles, a trompe l'oeil room is not the answer! You could consider painting tile panels and borders to be set amongst commercially produced plain white or coloured tiles. We use this decorative device time and time again.

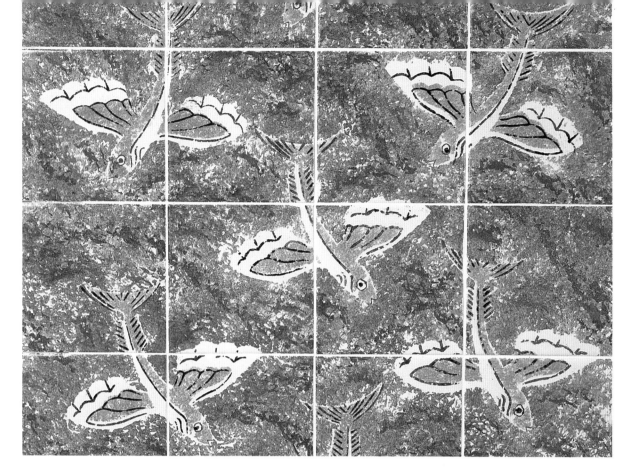

PART OF A SPONGED AND STENCILLED FLYING-FISH TILE PANEL.

A WHIMSICAL AND POETIC BUT
HIGHLY FUNCTIONAL TREATMENT OF
TILES BEHIND A WASHBASIN.

148

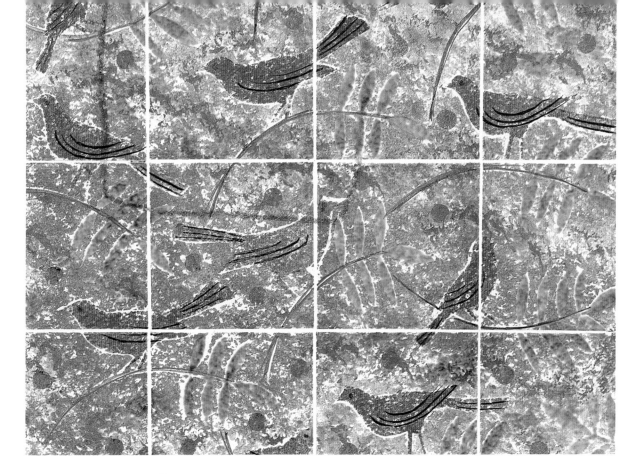

PART OF A SPONGED AND STENCILLED BIRD TILE PANEL.

ONE OF A SERIES OF SPONGED
AND STENCILLED TILE PANELS.
THIS ONE USES A FLOWER
MOTIF FEATURED IN MANY OF
OUR EARLY BLUE-AND-WHITE
PLATES, ENTITLED
'HYPERICUM', TOGETHER WITH
A HUMMINGBIRD AND COBALT-
PAINTED BACKGROUND.

OPPOSITE: FISH TILES USED IN
OUR BATHROOM AS BORDERS TO
MIRRORS WITH FISH PLATES.

A HAND-PAINTED TILE PANEL
WITH BORDER IN A BATHROOM —
WILD FLOWERS AND HOPS.

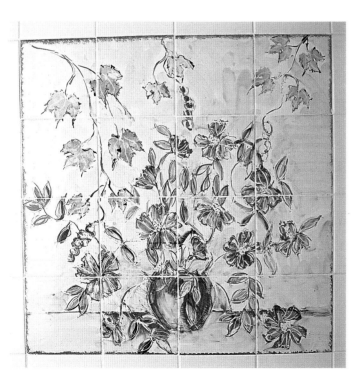

BUTTERFLIES, BIRDS AND WILD FLOWERS
SPONGED AND DELICATELY PAINTED
PROVIDE A HIGHLY FUNCTIONAL SOLUTION
TO THIS WOODEN KITCHEN.

'ASHMORE POND'. A HAND-PAINTED STUDY OF
DUCKS FOR A CUSTOMER LIVING IN THIS
PRETTY DORSET VILLAGE.

ONE OF A SERIES OF TILE PANELS OF SPONGED
AND STENCILLED FLOWERS.

SPONGED AND STENCILLED FISH ARE THE THEME FOR THIS BATHROOM.

A FEW STEEPLECHASE TILES MAKE AN INTERESTING DECORATIVE DETAIL
ON OUR FIREPLACE.

A MORE RECENT COLLECTION (PHOTOGRAPHED IN 1991) ON OUR RED
DRESSER SHOWS A COLOURFUL RANGE OF PAINTED AND SPONGED PLATES.

FURTHER READING

Ceramic Faults and their Remedies, Harry Fraser, A & C Black Ltd, 1986

Clay and Glazes for the Potter, D. Rhodes, Pitman, 1973 (Revised Edition)

The Craft of the Potter: A Practical Guide to Making Pottery, Michael Casson, BBC Publications, 1977

Electric Kilns and Firing, Harry Fraser, Pitman, 1979

Illustrated Dictionary of Practical Pottery, Robert Fournier, Van Nostrand Reinhold Co.

Pioneer Pottery, M. Cardew, Longman 1969, 1971 (New Edition)

A Potter's Book, B. Leach, Faber & Faber, 1945, 1976 (New Edition)

Pottery, Emmanuel Cooper, Macdonald Guidelines, 1976

Pottery and Ceramics, David Hamilton, Thames and Hudson, 1977

Pottery Without A Wheel, Keith Tyler, The Dryad Press, 1971

The Technique of Pottery, J. Colbeck, Batsford, 1975 (Revised Edition)

SUPPLIERS

This book is not a technical manual covering every aspect of pottery making – nevertheless we hope that we have explained clearly how to use the materials in our methods. Many of these techniques can be adapted to decorated other objects and surfaces as well. None of the materials or appartatus described here are difficult to get hold of or to use. In fact, the most important criteria we have employed in writing this book is that everything should be practical for anyone to do.

All pottery materials, glazes, clay and equipment from:

Pottery Crafts Ltd
Campbell Road
Stoke-on-Trent ST4 4ET
Tel: 0782 745000
Fax: 0782 746000

Drawing and design materials, stencil paper, majolica brushes and all other art materials from:

Frank Herring & Sons
27 High Street
Dorchester
Dorset DT1 1UP
Tel: 0305 267917 or 264449
Fax: 0305 250675

Useful addresses:

Crafts Council
44A Pentonville Road
Islington

London N1 9BY
Tel: 071-278 7700

Contemporary Applied Arts
43 Earlham Street
London WC2H 9LD
Tel: 071-836 6993

Craftsmen Potters Association
21 Carnaby Street
London W1V 1PH
Tel: 071-437 6781

Short courses:

Hinchcliffe and Barber
La Ferme de Cabourg
50630 Octeville L'Avenel
France
Tel: 010 33 33 54 63 12

Australia:

Walker Ceramics
55 Lusher Road
Croydon
Victoria 3136
Tel: (03) 725 7255
Fax: (03) 725 2289

Potters Warehouse
108 Oakes Road
Old Toongabbie
NSW, 2146
Tel: (02) 688 1777
Fax: (02) 636 3961

INDEX

Note: Page numbers in *italics*
denote illustrations

A

alumina *47*
animal designs
    see also individual animals
    Dorset Delft 13, *18*
    farmyard *86,* 108, *109, 110, 111*
    plates *141*
    zoo 134-7, *135,* 141
antelope design, plate *93*
apple designs *97*
    painting *98*
    plate *99*
artists' materials *11*
Ashmore Pond *152*
Atelier Martine 33-4
Athelhampton, tapestry of garden
   24
Audubon, John James 134

B

Barber, Harriet, seascape *116*
Beeton, Mrs 13-15
Bewick, Thomas 134
binders 73
bird designs *136*
    see also individual birds
    drawings *138-9*
    exotic 134-7, 141
    from coloured paper *138-9*
    plates, blue-and-white *41*
    tiles *37, 69, 149, 151*
biscuit firing 70, 72-3
blue-and-white pottery *12,* 13, *18,*
   22-3, 41, 42
    English 40-3
    tiles *37*
borders
    floral 43
    holly *19*
    seaweed *30-1*
Bournemouth, Russell-Cotes
   Museum

majolica *38*
    tile panel *146*
bowls, vine-leaf *12*
brushes 94

C

Carousel design *110*
Castelli, majolica from *38*
centre pieces 15
Chelsea Crafts Fair 27
children
    designs by 80-1, *80*
    plates for 19, *21*
china clay 46
Christmas designs 16-19
clay 46-7
    drying 65
    kneading 62-3
    preparing 62-3, *63*
    self-hardening 49
    storing 62
    unfired, decorating 84
clay bodies 47
cockerel designs *50-1, 106, 111,* 137
    plates 19, *20, 21, 115*
    step-by-step *112-15*
colours
    blues 40
    oxides 48-9
    for self-hardening clay 49
    stains 48-9
Cottage Pottery 40-1
country pottery *12*
cow creamers, sponged 41
cow design, plates *41*
Crafts Council 24
Cranborne Manor garden
    tapestry *97*
    tile panel *96*
Curtis, William 43

D

decoration
    applying, techniques 76-103
    overglaze 85

slip 84
    on unfired clay 84
delft 37, 40
    Dorset Delft 13, *18*
Deruta, majolica from 37
Devon Farm designs *109*
dinner services 15, *16*
    floral borders on 43
dishes, majolica *37, 39*
Dorset Delft 13, *18*
drawings 86-7, *86, 87, 124*
duck designs, plates *108, 140*
Dufy, Raoul 34

E

earthenware body, firing 72
earthenware clays 46
equipment 44-9, *46, 47*

F

fabrics
    African 137, 141
    fish *40, 81*
    tulip *17, 44-5*
faience 37
    platter *40*
farmyard designs *18, 86,* 108, *109,*
   110, 111
festive ware *10,* 13
    Christmas designs 16-19
firing 44, 46
    biscuit 70, 72-3
    glaze 74-5, *74*
fish designs
    drawings 86-7
    fabric *40, 81*
    plates 19, *81, 117, 121, 81*
    stencils for *88*
    step-by-step *118-21*
    tile panels *146, 147, 148, 150,*
   153
flocculents 73
flower designs *32, 104-5, 107,*
124-7
    see also individual flowers

borders 43
   from coloured paper *126*
   plates *12, 14*
      blue-and-white *43*
   sponging *91*
   tile panels *149, 151, 152*
   variety 124
flowers, in French garden *125*
fluxes *47*
food presentation 13-15, *13, 14, 15,* 17-19, *19*
France, tiles *145*
fruit designs *32*
   see also apple designs

G

Giverny, Monet's house 147
glass *47*
glazes 47-8
   firing 74-5, *74*
   increasing pick-up 73
   mixing 71
glazing 71-3, *71-3*
Gouda, tiles from *38*
Gould, John 134
Grant, Duncan 36
Grotto border plates 43
Grue, Aurelio, plate by *38*
gypsum 52

H

hen designs *50-1*
Hockney, David 33
Holland, tiles 144
holly design
   drawings *87*
   plates *19, 87*
hump moulds 50, 53
   casting from hollow mould 55
   making 56-8, *56-7*
hypericum designs
   plate *95*
   tile panel *149*

I

influences 30-43
inspiration 30-43
'istoriato' style 37

J

jewellery 24
jugs
   flower *6*
   rose *82*
   Tuscany *28*

K

kaolin 46
kilns 49, *49*
   alternative to 49
kneading 62-3

L

Lascaux cave paintings 137
linocuts *86*

M

majolica 37, *37-9,* 49
   decoration 85
   painting 96
materials 44-9
Monet, Claude, house at Giverny 147
Montelupa, majolica from *37*
moulds
   hollow, making 54-5
   hump 50, 53
      casting from hollow mould 55
      making 56-8, *56-7*
   making 52-8
mugs, sponged *12*

N

Nash, Paul 36
Nicholson, Ben 36

O

Omega Workshops 33
overglaze decoration 85, 96
oxides 47, 48-9

P

painting, freehand 96-7
partridge design, plate *89*
pattern *see* decoration
pheasant design, plate *78*
photocopying designs 87
Picasso, Pablo 33, 34
pinpricking *see* pouncing
Piper, John 36
plaster of Paris, mixing 52-3
plates and platters *12*
   announcement *10*
   antelope *93*
   apple *99*
   bird, blue-and-white *41*
   for children 19, *21*
   cockerel 19, *20, 21, 115*
   cow *41*
   duck *140*
   festive *10,* 13
   fish *19, 40, 81, 117, 121*
   flower *12, 14, 91*
   glaze firing 74, *74*
   glazing 73, *73*
   Grotto border 43
   holly-bordered *19*
   hypericum *95*
   majolica *38*
   making 50-65
      from mould *60-1,* 64-5, *65*
   moulds for 50, 52-8, *55*
   named 19
   partridge *89*
   pheasant *78*
   by Picasso *34*
   portrait 19
   rose *85*
   size and shape 53
   sizes 16
   sponged *82*
   steeplechase 13, *79*
   stoneware *29*
   template for 58
   tulip *15, 127, 130*
   vine-leaf *16*
   zebra *93*
Poiret, Paul 33-4
porcelain 46
portrait plates 19
Portugal, tiles 144

pouncing 97, 100-1, *101, 102-3*
  materials for *101*
Powell, Lady 27

R

Ravilious, Eric 36
rose design
  jug *82*
  platter *85*
  sponging *90*
Rotterdam, tiles from *38*

S

Salisbury Festival 27
Salisbury Museum, tile panel *59*
sea themes 116
seashore, as inspiration *35*
seaweed design *117*
  step-by-step *122-3*
  tiles *30-1, 123*
Seville, majolica workshop *39*
sgraffito 93, *93*
slab roller *47*
slip decoration 84
Spain, tiles 144
spongeware *91-2, 130*
  blue 40-1, *83*
  cow creamers 41
  plates and platters *10, 82*
sponging 76-7, 90, *90-1*
stains 48-9
steeplechase designs *131*
  dinner service 15, *16*
  plates and platters 13, *79*
  tiles *79, 154*

stencils 16-17, 19, 85, 88, *88-9*
stoneware 26
  platter *29*
stoneware clays 46
Sutherland, Graham 36

T

tapestries
  Athelhampton garden *24*
  three-dimensional 24
Tchalenco, Janice 26
  design *29*
templates, for plate 58
tile cutters *47,* 66-7
tile frame 67-8
tiles/tile panels *59,* 144-7
  bird *149, 151*
  blue-and-white *37*
  clays for 46-7
  Cranborne Manor garden *96*
  decorating 68
  delft 37
  Dorset Delft 13
  farmyard *69, 111*
  fish *146, 147, 148, 150, 153*
  flower *144, 149, 151, 152*
  French *145*
  glaze firing 74, *74, 75*
  glazing *72*
  making 66-8, *66-9*
  moulds for 50
  seaweed *123*
  seaweed border *30-1*
  steeplechase *79, 154*
  tin-glazed earthenware *38*
  tulip *127*

transfer printing 41-3
trek 100
trompe l'oeil effect 145-7
tulip designs *131*
  china *17*
  fabric *17, 44-5*
  plates *15, 127, 130*
  step-by-step *128-30*
  tile panel *127*
Turkey, tiles 144

U

underglaze decoration 96

V

vases, flower jug *6*
vegetable designs *32*
vine-leaf design *15*
  bowl *12*
  platters *16, 133*
  step-by-step *132*

W

weaving 22, 24
wedding designs 16
wedging 62
Wedgwood, floral plates 43

Z

zebra design *93*
zoo animal designs 134-7, *135,* 141